Musashi's D

The Way of the Lone Warrior

Endorsements

A Captivating and Enlightening Read!

I highly endorse *Musashi's Dokkodo: The Way of the Lone Warrior* by Dr. Bohdi Sanders. It is an exceptional book that explores the life and teachings of Miyamoto Musashi's last text, the *Dokkodo*. Sanders' storytelling style and vivid descriptions transport readers into Musashi's world, allowing us to accompany him on his journey of self-discovery and martial prowess. This book distills Musashi's wisdom into practical lessons that enhance our training and mindset. With historical context and a focus on Musashi's principles of life, it offers invaluable lessons extending beyond martial arts. I wholeheartedly recommend this captivating and enlightening read to any martial arts enthusiast.

GM Bill Staley
9th Dan in Black Belt Koshoryu Kenpo Karate
Deputy Sheriff and Professional Bodyguard

A Treasure Trove of Wisdom!

I scoff at how most martial artist, and some academics, reference the work of Japan's greatest duelist and strategist, while interpreting it to fit their narrative. Bohdi Sanders proves he is above this intellectual self-indulgence, as he ingeniously unveils the life-changing wisdom contained within the *Dokkodo*. Bohdi Sanders masterfully brings to light what we recognize as advantageous for our modern society. He takes Musashi's 21 principles and does more than just surgically dissect each one of these principles. He transforms each one into a treasure trove of wisdom, presented in such a way that it is relatable to anyone seeking to improve their life. I wholeheartedly recommend this remarkable book!

Soke Frank W. Dux
10 Degree Black Belt Whose Life is Depicted in the Movie Bloodsport.
Holds 14 Martial Arts World Records, Head of the Society of Black Dragons

Incredibly Inspiring, Motivating, with Valuable Insights!

I found this book to be brilliant! Its pages are filled with the importance of living a life of purpose and honor, not only in martial arts or combat, but in everyday life as well. *Musashi's Dokkodo* is incredibly inspiring, motivating, and filled with valuable insights for personal growth and self-improvement. This book gave me a renewed hunger to live life to the fullest! If you are seeking wisdom for navigating life's challenges, this book is a must read!

Janine Avanti
Award-Winning Actor and Author
World Champion Water Ski Racer and Champion Bodybuilder

Sanders Breathes New Life into Musashi's Principles!

Bohdi Sanders has once again proven his prowess in martial philosophy with his latest masterpiece. Known for his insightful and impactful works in the realm of martial arts literature, Sanders takes his readers on a transformative journey, seamlessly blending the ancient wisdom of Musashi with a contemporary perspective that resonates with today's audience.

Sanders, a highly respected martial artist, and prolific author, has an impressive body of work. In *Musashi's Dokkodo*, Sanders delves into the profound teachings of Miyamoto Musashi. What sets this book apart is Sanders' innovative interpretation of the *Dokkodo*. Sanders breathes new life into Musashi's principles, making them accessible and relevant to the challenges and aspirations of the 21st century.

Sanders skillfully weaves Musashi's timeless wisdom into a tapestry that speaks directly to everyone seeking personal growth, mental fortitude, and a deeper understanding of the martial way. The author's writing style is both engaging and enlightening.

One strength of Sanders' approach lies in his ability to bridge the gap between tradition and modernity. *Musashi's Dokkodo* is not merely a historical exploration, but a guide for the contemporary warrior, offering practical insights and actionable advice that can be applied in everyday life.

Sanders' deep respect for the root of martial arts is evident, yet he skillfully molds Musashi's principles into a relevant and empowering roadmap for navigating the complexities of today's world.

Musashi's Dokkodo is a triumph for Bohdi Sanders, showcasing his continued evolution as a martial arts philosopher. This book is a *must read* for anyone seeking a deeper understanding of martial arts philosophy, personal development, and the path to becoming a modern-day warrior. Sanders' ability to breathe new life into the *Dokkodo* ensures that this timeless wisdom will continue to inspire and guide martial artists for generations to come.

Grandmaster Ted Gambordella
10th Degree Black Belt, Martial Arts Hall of Fame inductee
and author of The Complete Book of Karate Weapons

A Playbook for Conquering Life!

Musashi's Dokkodo is a very relevant book which shows us how to incorporate Musashi's principles into the 21st century. I think this book is a playbook for living a life fully in our current times. The thoughts and ideas in this book are fantastic! *Musashi's Dokkodo* is a playbook for conquering life and living a happy existence. I highly recommend the book!

Master Allie Alberigo
8th Degree Black Belt in Ju Jutsu and Ninjustsu
and Founder of the LI Ninjutsu Centers

An Invaluable Guide, Brimming with Life Advice!

Bohdi Sanders delivers a faithful and intelligent exploration of the timeless principles outlined in *Musashi's Dokkodo*. Sanders adeptly captures the essence of Musashi's writings, offering readers a window into the warrior's profound insights on life. With acuity, Sanders addresses themes such as jealousy, respect for oneself, and the importance of self-discipline, all which resonate throughout Musashi's tenants. *Musashi's Dokkodo* is not merely a historical retelling, but an invaluable guide, brimming with life advice, which is sorely needed in contemporary society. I highly recommend this book for all those seeking direction in an ever-changing world. Sanders presents the information concisely and to the point, ensuring that the wisdom of Musashi is as impactful now as it was centuries ago.

Allen Woodman
Editor in Chief of International Martial Arts Magazine
6th Degree Black Belt and Author

Acclaimed Author, Dr. Bohdi Sanders, Never Seems to Disappoint!

Acclaimed author, Dr. Bohdi Sanders, never seems to disappoint, and his latest book, *Musashi's Dokkodo: The Way of the Lone Warrior*, presents readers with a look into the mind of one of the most accomplished warriors in history. Dr. Sanders' elaboration of Miyamoto Musashi's final writings provides every serious martial artist, or warrior, an amazing collection of guiding principles to learn, and live, the path of the Bushido code they have chosen. I highly recommend this book to everyone who chooses to truly live the martial way.

Soke Robert Cutrell
10th Degree Black Belt and Founder of ChunJiDo International
Robert holds a 6th Dan in Kempo and a 5th Dan in Nippon Jufitsu

Home Run-Out of the Park and Riveting!

Home run-out of the park and riveting! Once again, Dr. Sanders hits another home run. Today's warrior scholar continues to win battles by learning from the lessons of the past–whether on the battlefield or the business world, whether from a roaming ronin, like Miyamoto Musashi, or a battle-hardened general, like Sun Tzu. Here we follow the life of Musashi and learn from the timeless principles that became his way of life and made him successful, feared, and a legend. These principles are as relevant today as they were yester-year. Dr. Sanders captures the essence of those long ago lessons and brings them to the present so that we who want to thrive in life may learn from them. I truly applaud his efforts here.

Phil Torres, Colonel U.S. Marines, Retired
Vietnam Silver Star Medal Recipient
9th Degree Black Belt, Hanshi with 62 Years in Martial Arts

A Spectacular, Timeless Piece of Work!

Musashi's Dokkodo: The Way of the Lone Warrior by Bohdi Sanders, Ph.D. is a spectacular, timeless piece of work that everyone can learn from. A person can live a better life by applying any of these principles. This book is like an encyclopedia of knowledge on how to survive and walk the path of a warrior throughout your daily life. Being an Infantry Marine and a street cop, I understand and live life as a warrior, and Bohdi's work is right on point. The way of the warrior involves much more than the ability to fight or to defend yourself, but a roadmap to live your life by. I highly recommend everyone get a copy of this book! It could and will change your life if you apply even one of these principles.

Master Danny Lane
Highly Decorated Marine Awarded 2 Purple Hearts and Combat Action Medal
Decorated Police Officer, Martial Arts Master, Author-#1 book *Some Gave it All*

I was Moved to Deeply Reflect!

After reading Dr. Sanders' *Musashi's Dokkodo: The Way of the Lone Warrior*, I was moved to deeply reflect, from a Biblical perspective, upon Musashi's philosophy and Mr. Sanders' unfolding of the Dokkodo. Good writing should do this. It should stir you to find and/or strengthen your core values. This book has strengthened my personal relationship with Jesus Christ and for that, I am grateful. I encourage others to compare, for themselves, the teachings of Jesus and Musashi. I pray Musashi reached out to Jesus in his final moments and realized he was never aLONE.

Professor Karen Sheperd
8th Degree Black Belt, Black Belt Hall of Famer, Movie & Television Actress,
1st Generation Black Belt of Sifu Al Dacascos

Has the Power to Enrich the Lives of its Readers!

Musashi's Dokkodo: The Way of the Lone Warrior is a wonderfully written look at humanity through the eyes of a 17th century warrior. It gives evidence that humanity is, and always has been, according to how one chooses to view and react to the circumstances therein. This book has the power to enrich the lives of its readers, regardless of anyone's socioeconomic background. I am highly recommending this book to those who are searching for life's secrets; and to those who believe they have found them.

GM Sid Rayford
10th Degree Black Belt in Kobayashi Shorin-Ryu and
President of the American Martial Arts Teachers Organization

An Enlightening Must Read!

Dr. Bohdi Sanders is one of my all-time favorite authors, whose work always inspires with his resonating insights. His work, *Musashi's Dokkodo: The Way of the Lone Warrior*, is an enlightening must read, inspiring achievement of focus, honor, and excellence in life's challenging journey. 5 Stars!

Cheryl Kowalski
5th Degree Black Belt in American Tae Kwon Do
AOK Golden Greek Martial Arts Champion

I very Much Enjoyed Reading *Musashi's Dokkodo*!

When one wants to help themselves, whether spiritually, mentally, or with physical issues, or when one wants to help another person, inner peace is necessary. When one wants to feel peace or reach that the next step in a goal, inner peace is essential. Bohdi provides us with a real, historical view into how this is possible. I have experienced the ultimate highs and lows in life, so I know how true this is.

I very much enjoyed reading *Musashi's Dokkodo*! Bohdi Sanders is a very fine writer! I absolutely loved that he used real, historical facts of a great warrior to prove what is needed in our heart and mind, and in our pursuit of our dreams and happiness. Well done! I highly recommend this amazing book!

Dana Hee
Tae Kwon Do Olympic Gold Medal Winner
Award-Winning Stuntwoman, Survivalist

Musashi's Dokkodo

The Way of the Lone Warrior

Bohdi Sanders, PhD

Library of Congress Cataloging-in-Publication Data
Sanders, Bohdi, 1962-
Musashi's Dokkodo

ISBN – 978-1-937884-29-1

1. Martial Arts. 3. Karate. 3. Miyamoto Musashi. 4. Self-Defense.
5. Dokkodo. 6) Musashi. 7) The 21 Principles. 8) Title.

Kaizen Quest Publishing

Table of Contents

Acknowledgements

I want to thank Sifu Al Dacascos for his invaluable feedback and for taking the time to write the foreword for *Musashi's Dokkodo*. Sifu Al is a true friend and a valued resource who is always there when I need motivation, advice, or help. I am truly blessed to call Sifu Al my friend!

I also want to express my heartfelt appreciation to all the amazing people who took the time to read an advance copy of *Musashi's Dokkodo* and who honored me with their endorsements. My sincere appreciation goes out to each of the following:

Colonel Phil Torres
GM Frank W. Dux
Sifu Bill Staley
GM Ted Gambordella
Master Danny Lane
Master Allen Woodman
Professor Karen Sheperd
Soke Robert Cutrell
Master Allie Alberigo
GM Sid Rayford
Janine Avanti
Master Cheryl Kowalski
Dana Hee

And finally, I want to express my sincere appreciation to all my readers who have supported me over the years. Without you guys, I wouldn't be able to continue with my passion for writing and promoting the warrior lifestyle throughout the world. I have some of the most loyal readers in the world, and I greatly appreciate each and every one of you! Thank you so much for your continued support.

Foreword

In *Musashi's Dokkodo*, Dr. Bohdi Sanders embarks on a contemplative exploration of the timeless principles written by the legendary Japanese swordsman, Miyamoto Musashi. Unlike his other writings, the teachings in Musashi's *Dokkodo* go beyond the conventional notions of a warrior and reflect a more holistic philosophy of how he lived his life.

Dr. Bohdi Sanders masterfully delves into Musashi's final text, dissecting the principles of the *Dokkodo* with precision and insightful commentary, providing the reader with down-to-earth explanations concerning how each of the 21 principles can improve your life today. Sanders aptly explains this work as a reflection of Musashi's life, laying bare the principles held dear by this martial arts legend.

Dr. Sanders masterfully explains how the themes of independence, self-discipline, acceptance, detachment, personal responsibility, and self-confidence are found throughout the *Dokkodo*, and how important these concepts are to living a life of excellence in today's world. He also ingeniously explains how each applies to one's life today and compares the importance of each of the principles in Musashi's time as opposed to our current culture.

The *Dokkodo* imparts the essence of self-reliance, inner strength, and an unwavering pursuit of excellence to everyone who will study and apply the principles set forth by Miyamoto Musashi. While Musashi's teachings may seem rooted in the samurai ethos of the 17th century, their brilliance is their ability to still guide us in our modern, technologically driven world.

Dr. Sanders wisely points out that, while the principles encapsulated within the *Dokkodo* may not seamlessly align with the contemporary sensibilities of many people today, they still stand as a guide to developing and maintaining your personal excellence. In this meticulously crafted book, Sanders invites readers to confront life's challenges with a fearless heart, a determined spirit, and an unyielding commitment to excellence.

Whether or not you agree with every tenet, Musashi's principles offer a timeless framework for navigating the complexities of living a successful life. Sanders artfully bridges the distance between centuries with relevant and insightful commentary and does so in the straightforward and plain-spoken style that we have all come to expect from his writings.

Although certain principles may appear as though they cannot possibly apply to our modern world, Sanders' insight and distinguishing perspective guides the reader to find value in each principle. Sanders not only explains the value of each principle, but also shines a light on aspects of each that may not be obvious by simply reading the *Dokkodo* alone.

Dr. Sanders has taken a timeless, classic text and deeply expanded on it, transforming a short list of principles into a text that is an amazing guide to living a life of excellence and self-discipline. *Musashi's Dokkodo* is not only a fantastic guide for all martial artists, but is an outstanding handbook for anyone who wants to live a better life.

Embark on this journey with Dr. Bohdi Sanders and discover the enduring wisdom of the *Dokkodo* that transcends the ages, resonating as a source of inspiration for the modern seeker of wisdom and excellence. I enthusiastically endorse *Musashi's Dokkodo*! It is a gold mine for anyone seeking to improve their life.

Sifu Al Dacascos

Sifu Al Dacascos was inducted into the Black Belt Hall of Fame in 1977. He has been on the cover of over 185 National and International Martial Arts magazines and has won over 200 martial arts championships. Sifu Al is also the founder of the unique fighting art, Wun Hop Kuen Do, a system that incorporates Chinese and Filipino martial arts into the traditional KAJUKENBO system. He has trained many celebrities, including Eric Lee, Karen Sheperd, and his son, Mark Dacascos. His book, Legacy: Through the Eyes of the Warrior, was released in 2016, reaching #1 on Amazon in only four hours after its release.

Introduction

I choose to live by choice, not by chance.
Miyamoto Musashi

Miyamoto Musashi (1582-1645) is known as the greatest Japanese swordsman who ever lived. Musashi was a samurai before becoming a ronin and roaming the Japanese countryside and fighting in 60 duels over the years. Although Musashi doesn't give many details about his personal life, he does mention that he fought his first duel at the age of thirteen and spent the next 15 years traveling and fighting sword duels with other martial artists.

At the age of 30, he stopped traveling and dueling, and dedicated the rest of his life to seeking greater truths, teaching, meditation, and reflecting on the principles which lead to success in sword fighting. Musashi is regarded as a genius, both as a warrior, an artist, and as a teacher of the martial way.

Although he is widely considered the greatest swordsman ever in Japan, there are many critics who consider him to be the opposite of a warrior who lives in accordance with the ways of a true samurai or the ways of bushido, the way of the warrior. Musashi's critics, and those who strictly follow the ways of the samurai, consider some of Musashi's tactics to be cowardly and dishonorable.

To Musashi, winning was more important than the means that one used to ensure success. For example, he would use tactics such as delaying a fight or showing up late to irritate his opponent. He felt such tactics were simply good strategy and had nothing to do with honor; whereas his critics complained that such tactics lacked honor and decorum. His critics like to label many of Musashi's tactics and strategies as "winning by any means possible" and unbecoming for a samurai.

Personally, when it comes to a life-or-death battle, I side with Musashi. Rules are for sporting events. When you are facing an enemy who wants to kill you, you must win by any means necessary. Such things as decorum and honor have no place in a fight to the death. When it comes right down to it, you either walk away alive or you die. Musashi knew this and his strategies reflect this attitude.

Much of what we know about Musashi comes from tales which have been passed down over the centuries. What we do know is that Musashi was indeed a samurai and ronin, and he wrote six manuscripts over his lifetime: *Mirror on the Way of Combat* (1604), *Notes on Combat Strategy* (1638), *Combat Strategy in 35 Articles* (1641), *The Five-Direction Sword Pathways* (1642), *The Book of Five Rings* (1645), and *Dokkodo: The Path Walked Alone* (1645).

Out of all of Musashi's writings, *The Book of Five Rings* is his most well-known and treasured work. It, along with Sun Tzu's *The Art of War*, are the two most widely read and influential books among martial artists and strategists throughout the world.

As I mentioned earlier, Musashi stated that his first life-or-death duel occurred when he was 13 years old and that he successfully won 60 such duels in his lifetime. Although this information comes directly from Musashi, we ultimately do not have a lot of historical evidence concerning these duels. But there is historical evidence of Musashi writing the manuscripts mentioned above, although the original manuscripts have never been found.

The birthplace, birthdate, and actual family heritage have long been the basis for arguments and debates throughout Japan, and for our purposes here, none of those things matter. My purpose in this book is to expand on the 21 principles set forth in the *Dokkodo*; I will leave those other contentions to the historical experts.

What we do know is that after the age of 30, Musashi was more interested in his quest for higher awareness. This does not mean that he was no longer interested in martial arts. We know he had many martial arts students in his school, Niten Ichi Ryu.

After spending years refining his sword fighting skills and strategies, Musashi withdrew to the Reigando Cave in 1643 for a period of reflection, meditation, and to work on his last writings. One week before his death in 1645, he wrote the *Dokkodo* and gave his most revered student, Terao Magonojo, the copy of *The Book of Five Rings* and the *Dokkodo*.

The *Dokkodo*: *The Path Walked Alone*, was written just one week before Musashi's death and was the last known manuscript that he wrote. It contains 21 principles which Musashi wrote as he reflected on his life. Musashi's students of Niten Ichi Ryu call the *Dokkodo* "The Pledge" although it is not clear whether the *Dokkodo* was written as a reflection of his own life or as principles for his followers to implement in their lives. Either way, his students took it as a personal pledge to be adhered to in their personal lives.

Although Musashi is best known as a great swordsman, he is also known as a great strategist, teacher, artist, and philosopher. The teachings in the *Dokkodo* show he was a great believer in the importance of individuality, self-reliance, self-discipline, self-mastery, and detachment. He was a great believer in walking one's own path and not relying on others for support or validation. His philosophy can be summed up as the philosophy of personal responsibility, detachment, and self-discipline, all which we can use more of in today's entitlement culture.

Musashi encouraged people to take responsibility for their own decisions and actions. He refused to be influenced by the opinions of others or by society's expectations. He taught what we now call the philosophy of kaizen, constant, never-ending improvement, long before it became a widely known philosophy.

While *The Path Walked Alone* teaches individualism and personal responsibility, Musashi did not advocate complete isolation or giving up all interpersonal relationships. His teachings in the *Dokkodo* are more about maintaining one's individuality and not relying on others for guidance on how one should live his or her life. It is more about taking personal responsibility for developing excellence in one's own life and living by your own rules.

It is about embracing self-reliance, cultivating inner strength, personal responsibility, and the constant, never-ending pursuit of excellence in whatever one does in life. Musashi taught us to face all of life's challenges with a fearless heart, a determined spirit, and a constant desire for excellence in all that you do.

While you may not agree with all of Musashi's teachings, please keep in mind that these teachings originated in the first half of the 17th century and from years spent living as a ronin. He faced death repeatedly in situations where even the slightest mistake could have cost him his life. While some of these teachings may not be as applicable in today's world as they were in the 1600s, hopefully you will find the strategies, and my interpretations, useful for your life today.

This is just a brief summary of Musashi's life and is not meant to be an in-depth look at his 63 years on this earth. There are several really good, in-depth books which delve into the historical Musashi.

If you are interested in knowing more about his life, I recommend that you check out some of the more historical books, along with his other writings.

My purpose with this book is not necessarily to discuss the historical Musashi, but rather to delve into the wisdom contained in the *Dokkodo,* and to expand on that wisdom, making it relevant for today's world. I will leave the historical information and debates concerning the specifics of Miyamoto Musashi's life to the experts in Japanese history.

As with all my books, I am interested in the strategies and wisdom that are universal and can be applied to our life to empower and motivate us to live a better, more disciplined life today. Aspire not simply to read *Musashi's Dokkodo*, but to apply the wisdom contained in this book to your current life. If you do, you will discover that you will become more successful and more disciplined.

Dokkodo
The Way of the Lone Warrior

1) Accept everything just the way it is.

2) Do not seek pleasure for its own sake.

3) Do not, under any circumstances, depend on a partial feeling.

4) Think lightly of yourself and deeply of the world.

5) Be detached from desire your whole life long.

6) Do not regret what you have done.

7) Never be jealous.

8) Never let yourself be saddened by a separation.

9) Resentment and complaint are appropriate neither for oneself or others.

10) Do not let yourself be guided by the feeling of lust or love.

11) In all things have no preferences.

12) Be indifferent to where you live.

13) Do not pursue the taste of good food.

14) Do not hold on to possessions you no longer need.

15) Do not act following customary beliefs.

16) Do not collect weapons or practice with weapons beyond what is useful.

17) Do not fear death.

18) Do not seek to possess either goods or fiefs for your old age.

19) Respect Buddha and the gods without country on their help.

20) You may abandon your own body but you must preserve your honor.

21) Never stray from the way.

Principle 1
Accept everything just the way it is.

In this principle, Musashi urges us to accept everything in life as it is. Many have challenges where this is concerned. In life, there are some things that you simply have no power to change. It does no good to sit around and wish that those things were different or to worry about how those things will affect your life.

When it comes to things which are beyond your control, it is best to simply accept them as they are and then decide how you can best use them, or work around them, to your advantage.

No matter how much you would like for those things to be different, worrying about them won't change anything. Wishing that those things were different, or worrying about them, only adds stress to your life. This doesn't change anything or make anything better; but in reality, it makes your life worse.

Worrying about the way things are, or wishing that things could be different, never improves your situation. There are things in this world that you have the power to change for the better, and there are things you can do nothing about. To have peace in your life, you must be able to discern the difference between the two, controlling what you can control and accepting those things which you can't control.

If something is not how you would like it to be, and you have some control over it, then take action to change it. When you have the power to make things in your life better, then you should absolutely step up, take that responsibility, and make the specific changes that will improve your life.

On the other hand, there are many things which you have no control over. By accepting these things as they are, you can let go of any worry, stress, or negative emotions connected to those things. No matter how much you worry about those things, stress over them, or want them to be different, you simply can't change them. These are the things which you must accept as they are.

When it comes to the things which are outside of your control, you have two choices–accept them as they are or continue to worry and stress over them, turning a blind eye to the reality of the situation. Accepting everything just the way it is, then developing a strategy to deal with those things, increases your inner peace and gives you a certain amount of control over your life.

Refusing to accept things as they are does the exact opposite; it adds stress to your life and gives you a feeling that your life is spinning out of control. Not accepting things as they are is like fighting a battle that cannot be won. Sun Tzu, in his book, *The Art of War*, taught us, "If a battle cannot be won, do not fight it."

When you fight a battle that cannot be won, you gain nothing; you are wasting your time and energy. No matter what strategy you use, or how hard you try, you will never win that battle because it simply cannot be won. This is an exercise in frustration and futility.

Think about it this way. If you have a large square peg and you are trying to fit it into a smaller, round hole, it doesn't matter how much time you spend trying to make it fit into that hole; it just won't fit. You can accept that fact or you can continue in vain to try to change it. Trying to change it will only lead to frustration, waste your time, and makes you look foolish to those around you.

Consider the Serenity Prayer, "God, grant me the *serenity* to accept the things I cannot change, the courage to change the things I can, and the wisdom to know the difference." Serenity is basically the calm peace that you have once you accept something as it is and move on. You must accept the things that you cannot change in a calm, tranquil way, and continue with your life, improving yourself daily despite whatever is going on around you.

The last part of the Serenity Prayer is also very important. If you don't have the wisdom to know what you can change and what you cannot change, then you will end up accepting things that you don't have to accept, and trying to change things that you have no power to change. This is not a strategy for a successful or peaceful life!

There are many things which you can change. You can change your self-talk, your speech, your attitude, your habits, your behavior, your mindset, your lifestyle, your relationships, your thoughts, your actions, etc. This is not an exhaustive list by any means.

Most of the things that are in your control have to do with you personally. You don't have control over how other people act, what they say, what they think, their actions, their opinions, or how they live their life. Trying to control other people will lead to frustration and disrupt your inner peace, even if your intentions are good.

Always remember, you have no control over anyone except yourself.

When you stop and think about it, you have very little control over anything outside of your personal life. But even though we have no control over certain things or certain events, we do have control over our responses and our thoughts concerning those things. Always remember, when something is outside of your control, there is still an area associated with it that is within your control–how you think about it and how you respond to it. This holds true of everything which is outside of your control.

Consider a newscast about some horrible natural disaster. Of course, you have no control over what is happening, but you do have a choice about whether to accept things as they are, and not allow them to negatively affect you, or to allow them to stress you out, worry you, and upset you. Either way, things are what they are. Your only decision is will you choose to respond positively or will you allow what has happened to negatively affect you.

You must understand what is in your sphere of control and what is outside of your sphere of control. If something is inside your sphere of control, that is where your focus should be. If something is outside of your sphere of control, then you should accept it as it is and move on from there.

Turning a blind eye to the truth does not change the truth. The truth does not simply go away or change because of your refusal to accept it or acknowledge it. The truth is simply the truth; things are what they are. Refusing to accept the way things are only handicaps you. If you refuse to see a situation for what it is, how can you effectively deal with that situation?

You must first accept the situation as it is, then you can decide how to best respond to it. Once you accept that things are what they are, then you can start to develop a strategy for how to best deal with what is going on. Stop complaining about what has happened and make a plan to respond to it. Complaining only makes everything worse for you and those around you. Musashi knew this and addressed complaining in another principle of the *Dokkodo*. I will discuss this in more detail later.

Dr. Wayne Dyer taught, "Acceptance means no complaining, and happiness means no complaining about the things over which you can do nothing." If you are complaining about the way things are, you are neither accepting what is, nor spending your time developing a strategy for dealing with those things.

Complaining about how things are changes nothing and never makes anything better. When you complain, you are actually adding stress to your life and weakening your spirit. Research has shown that complaining actually shrinks the area of your brain that is critical to problem solving. This means that when you complain, you are only making things worse for yourself.

Accepting things as they are is the first step to overcoming any negative side effects of what is happening. Acceptance is the key to successfully dealing with whatever is happening in your life or in the world around you. Refusing to accept how things are keeps you stuck in a fantasy world of denial.

Some people seem to believe that if they ignore a negative situation, it will somehow magically go away. That is a refusal to accept reality. Ignoring reality doesn't change what is happening. It only robs you of the chance to either use what is happening to your advantage or to develop a sound strategy to offset the negative consequences of what is happening. Musashi knew this.

Lao Tzu, the author of *The Tao Te Ching*, stated, "Life is a series of natural and spontaneous changes. Don't resist them; that only creates sorrow. Let reality be reality. Let things flow naturally forward in whatever way they like."

The *Tao* states we should let things flow naturally forward in whatever way they like, but the truth is you have no choice in the matter. Things outside of your control will move forward as they will, whether you like it or not, or whether you accept them or not. You have no control over them whatsoever.

What you do have control over is whether you accept the way things are. You must accept what is before you can decide how to respond to what is happening. Don't wish for them to be anything other than what they are, as that is an exercise in futility. See things as they truly are, then respond to them or just move on.

Consider the theory of amor fati, a love of fate. Essentially, this is a deep acceptance of whatever happens in your life. The German philosopher, Friedrich Nietzsche, stated, "That one wants nothing to be different, not forward, not backwards, not in all eternity. Not merely to bear what is necessary, still less to conceal it, but to love it." This is a very stoic attitude towards things which are outside of your control. If you develop this kind of attitude towards the things that happen in your life, you will have much less frustration.

The refusal to accept the various things that happen in your life leads to a life full of frustrations, stress, irritation, and anger, none of which are conducive to a life of inner peace and rational thought. If you allow the things outside of your control to continually get to you and put you into a fit of anger and frustration, you will continually distract yourself from your larger goals.

I know people who allow something as meaningless as some stranger cutting them off in traffic to completely rob them of their inner peace. They will go into a rage of frustration and anger because of the actions of someone else, instead of simply accepting the fact that there are many jerks in this world.

You have no control over how someone else acts, much less how they drive. Realize that when you allow some guy's rude driving to frustrate you and make you angry, it doesn't add anything positive to your life. It certainly does not matter to the other guy whether you like his driving. Your anger and frustration mean absolutely nothing to him. You are not ruining his drive or affecting him in any way. It is only affecting you negatively by changing your mood, raising your blood pressure, and getting you all worked up.

What you must realize is you have a choice concerning how you will respond to those kinds of situations. Instead of allowing something that is completely out of your control to affect you, you could choose to laugh and say, "Wow! Look how that clown is driving." Or simply ignore his rudeness altogether and be thankful that you were able to react to his driving without incident.

Another example along the same line is when some guy feels the need to flip you the bird and start screaming and yelling at you as you are driving. You can allow his immature behavior to make you angry and respond in kind, which again, only affects you negatively, or you could simply ignore him and go on about your day. If you feel you must physically respond to him, you could do what my wife does and wave at him like a little kid at a parade with a big smile on your face, although this choice would not be my recommendation.

The point is, you have no control over the actions of other people, so just accept things as they are and move on with your life. Let go of your need to respond negatively to the words or actions of others. Let go of your need to be in control of things outside of your sphere of control. When you get right down to it, you don't have a choice; you have no control over those things.

Remember, you have no power to change anything outside of your sphere of control. Your choices are to accept things as they are, respond to them and move on, or to wish things were not as they are, which creates stress and problems in your life. In addition, you don't even have to respond to most things which are outside of your sphere of control. Just observe what is happening, resolve not to allow it to negatively affect you, and move on with your life.

Trying to control things which are outside of your control is a sure-fire way to disrupt your inner peace and sidetrack your day. Yet this is how many people choose to live their life; they choose to allow mostly meaningless things to anger or frustrate them, and to disrupt their inner peace.

Stop expecting everything to go exactly as you want it to go. In most cases, this is the exception rather than the rule. Just think about how many days you have had when everything went according to how you planned it, with no surprises or hassles at all. If you are like most people, those days are few and far between. Stop having unrealistic expectations and simply decide to accept things as they are and move on with a smile.

If you do this, you will have much more peaceful days, fewer frustrations and anger, and more inner peace. You will also find that you will get more things done because you are refusing to allow things outside of your control to sidetrack you. You won't waste precious time on meaningless anger and frustration.

Determine to live your life by the Serenity Prayer, "God grant me the *serenity* to accept the things I cannot change, the courage to change the things I can, and the wisdom to know the difference." Make "it is what it is," your response to everything that you cannot change or control. Accept everything just the way it is.

Truth is not what you want it to be; it is what it is,
and you must bend to its power or live a lie.
Miyamoto Musashi

Principle 2
Do not seek pleasure for its own sake.

The second principle in Musashi's *Dokkodo* seems a little odd until you give it some thought. Seeking pleasure solely for pleasure's sake has many drawbacks and hidden traps.

Think about how many people started out simply enjoying the pleasure of drugs, alcohol, or smoking, only to have their favorite pleasure ensnare them in an addiction which ended up costing them in many ways. Therapists today are booked solid with people who are addicted to one pleasure or another.

These people didn't start out seeking pleasure for its own sake; they started out just using alcohol or drugs with their friends on a crazy night out. Soon, they were partying every Friday and Saturday night without giving it any thought.

A couple of nights a week soon turned into using alcohol or drugs throughout the week whenever they had a bad or a stressful day. Before they know it, they are drinking or using drugs every day and their life revolves around their addiction. In fact, they get so addicted to their chosen "pleasure" that their mind is pretty much focused on that "pleasure" during most of their waking hours.

Soon they stop doing the other things that they used to find pleasure in doing. Where they used to enjoy exercising, working out, or practicing martial arts, they now skip those pleasurable activities for the "pleasure" of drinking or getting high.

Instead of feeling good about themselves, they find themselves isolated from their friends and family, and chasing the "pleasures" which they now crave more than anything else. What started out as a way to have fun with their friends has now enslaved them. It was once a small part of their overall life, but now they chase these fleeting "pleasures" solely for *their own sake.*

As they isolate themselves more and more, their genuine desires fall by the wayside, distracted by these false "pleasures" which now fully entangle their mind and body with their short-lived dopamine fix. They can never get enough of their new pleasure; it dominates their mind during every waking moment.

It seems to them that their lives somehow changed overnight. The people, goals, and pleasures which used to mean so much to them, are now not so important and take a backseat to their new addiction. Now, their new pleasure has become more of a necessity than an enjoyment. And it all started simply by seeking pleasure for its own sake.

Unfortunately, this overview of seeking pleasure for its own sake is all too real for many people today. Recent studies found that over 20 million people in the United States alone deal with what is now known as a substance use disorder. Most of us are more familiar with this being known as an addiction to either alcohol or drugs.

Keep in mind that this number only includes alcohol and drugs. Seeking pleasure for its own sake includes much more than alcohol and drugs. Today, the pleasures that ensnare people range from addictions to food and sugar to addictions to using social media. Some people are addicted to sex and others to using cell phones. The pleasures that people seek are almost limitless.

Musashi knew that seeking pleasure for its own sake could take over one's mind if one was not careful and disciplined. This does not mean that Musashi was against having fun or enjoying the good things that life has to offer; that is not what he is saying at all.

Musashi enjoyed painting, poetry, tea ceremonies, meditation, and teaching others, along with his martial arts practice. I am sure that he enjoyed good food and drink just as much as other people did, but he kept his priorities straight. He did not seek pleasure simply for its own sake; disciplining himself, he enjoyed his pleasures in moderation. Musashi controlled his own life, and he refused to allow external pleasures to control him.

When you overstep the bounds of moderation, even the greatest pleasures cease to please. Think about it like this. If you have not had any of your favorite dessert in a couple of months, you may start to crave it. So, you go to the store and buy all the ingredients to make your favorite dessert. You can't wait to sink your teeth into the first bowl of pudding, piece of pie, or cake.

When it is ready, you immediately get a large serving of it. It does indeed hit the spot, so you decide to have more. Then later that day you have another serving of it, but somehow it does not taste quite as good as the first couple of servings. By the time the dessert is gone, you are definitely not craving anymore of it for a while.

Too much of anything causes you to enjoy that specific pleasure less. If you sit down and eat an entire cherry pie at one sitting, by the time you get to that last piece, it will not be a pleasure, but unpalatable. Moderation is important in all your pleasures. Pleasure should not cause you to lose sight of your true goals.

Enjoy pleasure when it comes, but never allow yourself to get emotionally, mentally, or physically attached or addicted to it. Pleasure, in and of itself, will never completely fulfill you; it is always temporary. It doesn't matter if it is alcohol, drugs, sugar, food, or social media, the joy of that dopamine rush, which you get from whatever enjoyment you choose, will be temporary. Never allow temporary pleasures to control your life!

True happiness comes from working towards something meaningful in your life; it is a by-product of working to achieve something greater than yourself or your own individual amusements. Viktor Frankl, the author of *Man's Search for Meaning*, wrote, "When a person can't find a deep sense of meaning, they distract themselves with pleasure."

This is essentially what Musashi was trying to get across to us. A man should have a more profound goal in his life, something greater than simply living for his own personal enjoyment.

We know that Musashi's greatest passion was his martial arts training, but that was not his only passion. As I mentioned, he also enjoyed art, poetry, teaching, and meditation. He believed that a true martial artist should be well-balanced. In addition, he also believed that you should live a disciplined life, doing nothing which is not useful.

We all need time to relax and enjoy life, and there are countless activities and past times which we can enjoy in today's world. While there is nothing wrong with playing golf or tennis, your personal pleasures should be enjoyed in moderation. Anything in excess can become problematic in your life.

Another way of saying, "Do not seek pleasure for its own sake," is "don't let any of your pleasures control you." Enjoy what life offers, but keep your priorities straight. Make sure your pleasures do not dominate your thoughts and start controlling you to the detriment of your true goals and values.

Maintain control over the things that you enjoy; never allow them to control you. Once a chosen pleasure starts to control your thoughts, or you find it is always on your mind, that should be a big red flag for you that it is becoming too important. Be disciplined and always maintain control of your own life. Keep your mind free from distractions and focus on higher goals.

When anything outside of you starts to demand too much of your attention, that is when you need to put a stop to it, or at least to put it on the back burner for a while. Worldly pleasures are here for us to enjoy, not for us to cater to them. If your chosen pleasure starts to dominate your thoughts, when you should be focused on other goals, you know it is having an unhealthy hold on your mind. The pursuit of pleasure can distract you from what is truly important in life and can lead to a lack of discipline and self-control.

As you read the *Dokkodo*, you will find that there are certain themes which have a common thread through most of Musashi's principles. You will notice that most of the principles are based on self-discipline, detachment, self-control, and mindfulness.

Controlling your desire to seek pleasure simply for its own sake takes self-discipline. We all enjoy certain pleasures in life, and there is nothing wrong with enjoying the good things that life offers. But you must maintain your discipline and self-control. Allow nothing to enslave you.

You should free yourself from anything that controls your mind or your life. When you feel you are seeking a certain pleasure too much, or that a specific pleasure is taking up too much of your mental or emotional energy, it is time for you to step up and take back control of your life.

As Aristotle put it, "Moderation in all things." Too much of anything can become a problem in your life. Focus on moderation in all your pleasures. This takes discernment and good judgment. As I mentioned, certain pleasures can become a habit before you know what is happening, unless you use discernment in your life. This means that you must live a mindful life.

If you are mindful as you go through life, you will continually monitor your time. You will know when you are doing something too much, or thinking about it too much, and it is interfering with your higher goals or personal values.

Recognize that true happiness does not come from meaningless pleasures or external things. Happiness comes from inside you and from living a meaningful life. Once you are living the life that you were meant to live, you will find that you get enjoyment from the simpler things in your life. These things will give you greater enjoyment and satisfaction than the type of pleasures which often become addicting.

Furthermore, if you have specific goals and a higher purpose in life, you will find that you don't have time to waste on seeking pleasure for its own sake. Your pleasure will then be more of a reward for your hard work, and you will enjoy those pleasures more. When you are less attached to specific a pleasure, you will be more detached concerning how you enjoy your life. You will find enjoyment in almost everything you do.

Have a purpose which is larger than yourself. This is what Viktor Frankl, meant by, "When a person can't find a deep sense of meaning, they distract themselves with pleasure." You must find the deeper meaning in life. Why are you here? What is your true purpose?

I am sure that you have heard the expression, when you do what you love for a living, you will never work a day in your life. This is what it means to have a deep sense of meaning or a higher purpose in life. When you are focused on your higher goals, those goals become your purpose. And when you are doing what you love, you are enjoying your life across the board, not just occasionally when you are seeking other pleasurable activities.

Also, when you have a deeper purpose in life, you will avoid making impulse decisions because you will be more mindful and focused. The pleasures that distract so many other people won't be tempting to you, as you have more important things on your mind. You will have higher goals to focus on and you will find that you are getting more enjoyment in working towards your higher goals than if you were seeking other external pleasures.

In addition, make sure that you don't allow your higher goals to completely control your mind either. That is a workaholic. It doesn't matter what it is, refuse to allow anything external to have a hold on your mind. You must be the captain of your own life; refuse to allow anything or anybody to take the helm from you.

Refuse to allow any pleasure to dominate your mind or your time. It doesn't matter whether it is alcohol, drugs, food, sex, social media, or your favorite hobby, refuse to allow anything to rule your life. Remember what Lao Tzu taught: "Excessive indulgence in sensory pleasure can dull our ability to appreciate the simple joys in life."

You must know what your purpose in life is and keep it foremost in your mind, while at the same time maintaining balance in your life. Know what your goals are and design your life around them. Discipline yourself and get your priorities straight!

Remember what Democritus wrote: "The brave man is he who overcomes not only his enemies but his pleasures." Don't allow any pleasure, no matter how much you enjoy it, to control your life. You must control your pleasures, not allow your pleasures to control you.

Once you know what your priorities are, and your life revolves around your true purpose, then you can enjoy life's pleasures in moderation without seeking them for their own sake. You must stay in control of your life; don't allow anything or anybody else to dictate how you will live your life or what you will do.

Do nothing which is of no use.
Miyamoto Musashi

Principle 3
Do not, under any circumstances, depend on a partial feeling.

In principle three, Musashi is strongly urging us to never act on strong emotions or partial information without giving the situation rational thought. This is great advice for any situation in which you find yourself.

Acting on powerful emotions is a perfect example of depending on a partial feeling. A powerful emotion is not only a partial feeling, but a temporary feeling as well. Just think about how many grave mistakes you would have made if you had acted on your emotions every time you were angry or very hurt about some situation. It is rarely wise to act on pure emotion without giving the situation some rational thought.

Depending on a partial feeling is acting on momentary, highly emotional thoughts without taking the time to really give the situation some rational thought. Thoughts, just like emotions, come and go. Think about how many times you have had irrational thoughts which, if acted on, would have caused you some major problems or even cost you a relationship.

Many times, your heart and mind have feelings and thoughts that are not rational or complete. Your initial thoughts and emotions will steer you wrong more times than not, if you don't slow down and think rationally. When you are dealing with an important decision or a dangerous situation, it is vital that you slow down and give the issue some time and clear-headed thought before you act.

Your immediate, strong feelings should almost always be measured by objective, rational thought. When you have a powerful urge to act on pure emotion, stop yourself and think rationally. The prisons are full of people who simply acted on pure emotion without stopping and thinking about the whole situation.

Think about it. If you are in a pub with your wife and some obnoxious drunk comes up to your table and starts making inappropriate comments to your her, your first thought might be to knock him on his butt. This would be acting out of pure emotion and a partial feeling, without giving the situation any rational thought. That is reacting, not responding!

There are many people in prison right now for that exact same kind of reaction. They allowed their temper to dictate their actions instead of slowing down, thinking, and de-escalating the situation. Think about this. The guy immediately jumps up, pushes the drunk backwards away from the table, exchanges some choice words, and then the drunk throws a punch. Being drunk, his punch is easily blocked and countered, but the counter punch knocks him down and he lands awkwardly, injuring his neck or back.

The police show up and arrest the man for assault and battery, costing him time off his job and thousands of dollars to hire a lawyer and deal with the consequences of the whole situation. A few weeks later, while going about his business, not even thinking about that situation anymore, the man gets a letter from the drunk's attorney suing him for his injuries.

Now he not only has to go to trial, but he is being sued in addition to the assault and battery charges, costing him even more money and time off work. He ends up praying that he doesn't go to prison or lose his home because of this ridiculous situation.

Acting, or depending, on a partial feeling, or on pure emotion, is rarely a good idea. A ridiculous situation can quickly escalate, causing things to become much worse than you ever imagined.

If the guy in the example above had used some rational wisdom in that situation, he would have stood up and defended his wife, while realizing that he was dealing with some drunk. Instead of getting physical, he could have de-escalated that situation with just a few well-thought-out words and sent the drunk on his way, while he and his wife enjoyed the rest of his night.

While this is an extreme example of acting on a partial feeling, this is not an uncommon situation. When you rely solely on a one-sided perspective and/or powerful emotions, more often than not, you will misjudge the situation, which will lead to a less than optimal outcome.

If you are not sure that you have all the information that you need, it is best to take the time to gather more facts before you act. When there is a lot riding on your decision, you need to have as much information as possible. Acting on incomplete information or a partial feeling is simply not wise.

Let's go back to the example of the obnoxious drunk in the pub. If the man defending his wife's honor allowed his emotions to dictate his actions, he may have let his temper cause him to forget his self-defense skills and reacted wildly. Acting on emotions instead of being in complete control, he may have missed the fact that the drunk guy had his hand on a knife that he was ready to pull. Instead of going to jail, the guy could have taken a trip to the hospital, or worse.

There are always worse case scenarios when it comes to acting without being in complete control of your mind and emotions. Emotions are fickle; they change constantly. Many times, acting on a partial or incomplete feeling is worse than doing nothing at all.

A partial feeling lacks conviction and commitment. You cannot have total commitment or complete conviction if you are not completely sure about what you are doing or why you are doing it. When you act under such circumstances, you are acting half-heartedly.

In Musashi's case, acting on a partial feeling could have cost him his life. Musashi fought over 60 duels with a sword. These were not sparing sessions, but rather life-or-death fights. Each one was an extremely serious affair. He had to be completely committed to his cause and have as much reliable and comprehensive information about his opponents and the terrain as possible.

If he had moved on strong emotion or partial information, not taking the time to consider his situation, it could have been catastrophic for him. He had to control his emotions and only act after he had given the situation a lot of thought and preparation.

If you have read *The Book of Five Rings*, you already know that Musashi not only did not act on partial information, but he did everything in his power to cause his opponents to act on a partial feeling or raw emotions. He actively attempted to anger or trick his opponents. Musashi knew that if he could get inside his opponent's mind, he had the fight won.

While acting on a partial feeling may not be a life-or-death situation for you (although is certainly could be), it can still cost you a lot of grief. If you invest thousands of dollars on a partial feeling about a stock or a business, it could end up costing you dearly. No rational person would risk his or her money on a partial feeling without doing their due diligence.

Don't allow laziness or complacency to cause you to act without doing your homework. With the information that we literally have at our fingertips with the internet, there is pretty much nothing that we cannot research and make an informed decision on today. You simply need to discipline yourself and take the time to research the valuable information that you need.

Many people act on partial feelings or incomplete information simply because it is easier than taking the time to study and make an informed decision. Acting on a partial feeling is no different from gambling. A wise person wouldn't gamble with his life or his family's finances, yet many people do just that every single day because they do not want to slow down and gather the information needed to make an informed decision.

They act out of a random impulse instead of giving their situation some rational thought and acting on well-researched, complete information. Then they wonder why things never seem to work out for them.

Musashi expressed how important it is in every situation to make sure you are acting rationally. He did not say that you should not depend on partial feelings in serious situations; he said do not, *under any circumstances*, depend on a partial feeling.

The wise man will think rationally, no matter what he is doing. There is rarely a circumstance where you should throw caution to the wind and just act without giving what you are about to do some rational thought.

There are people today who are paralyzed from the neck down because they acted carelessly and dove into water without rationally thinking about what they were about to do. They acted on a partial feeling, thinking that it was hot and that the cool water would feel great. So, they jumped in without giving it any serious thought, not realizing that the water was too shallow or that there may be boulders or old tree stumps under the water.

Always maintain a clear and balanced mindset. Control your emotions instead of allowing your emotions to control you. Acting on a partial feeling means you are unsure or indecisive. If you are unsure about an action, then you are not totally convinced that your decision is right. And if you are not totally convinced that your decision is right, you will not be completely committed to the action which you are about to take.

In hand-to-hand combat, which is how Musashi lived the first half of his life, you must be completely convinced that you are taking the right action. If you are unsure, it will affect your technique because your mind won't be totally focused. This is not the situation you want to find yourself in when you are fighting for your life!

While you may not find yourself fighting for your survival, life is full of serious decisions. It is unwise to act on a partial feeling. You must consider different perspectives and look at the all the angles of the issue at hand. Do your homework and understand the situation completely.

If you find you are not sure about what to do, simply wait and do nothing until you feel secure about your decision. Many times, you will find that doing nothing, waiting, and observing is the best answer to the situation. Doing nothing is better than making a wrong decision and can save you a lot of hassles or heartbreak. Avoid impulsive behavior!

Have you ever wondered why grocery stores put candy bars and sodas right in front of the checkout counters? They want you to act on impulse so they can get more of your money. Supermarket managers know that you most likely did not come to the store to buy candy bars or a 16-ounce bottle of Coke.

If they had placed these things randomly in the aisles, you most likely would not have put them in your cart. But they place them in front of the counter, so you will see them while you wait in line, hoping you will buy them without giving it much thought. They count on your impulsive behavior to cause you to spend more money.

Acting on impulse is doing the exact opposite of giving a situation some rational thought. You may be unsure whether you should do something, so instead of waiting and thinking about it, you simply bite the bullet and act.

Salesmen understand this concept all too well. That is why many salesmen will pressure you to make a quick decision; they do not want you to take the time to think about your finances or whether you actually need their product. They want you to sign on the dotted line quickly, so you won't think about it and back out of the deal.

Anytime someone is pressuring you to make a fast decision about something that will affect your financial situation, or some other important aspect of your life, it is usually best to slow down and take some time to think about it for a while. If a salesman is adamant about his offer only being available if you buy now, simply tell him you will pass. I assure you, more times than not, he will give you the same deal later. After all, his job is to sell his products, not to be stubborn with his customers.

Principle three is urging you to be self-controlled instead of impulsive or acting without being sure that it is the right move for you to make. Make your decisions on a complete understanding of the situation after examining all the various angles and aspects of your position.

Whether you are relaxing on vacation, getting ready to invest your life savings, or in a serious life-or death situation, there is never a good time to depend on partial feelings or incomplete information. Always listen to your intuition! Your inner spirit will let you know whether or not what you are doing is right or whether you need to take some more time to think about it.

Acting when you are unsure that you are doing the right thing will cause you to have the feeling of butterflies in your stomach. This nervous feeling will let you know you are taking a risk and that maybe you should pause and gather more information before you act.

When you are sure about what action to take, you will feel a calm, secure feeling inside, not butterflies. Think about it. If you put a large amount of money on a number on a roulette wheel, how do you feel inside? Butterflies, right? But if you make a well-thought-out decision about your son's education, you don't feel those butterflies; you have a calm, secure feeling about your decision.

There are things which you can prepare for beforehand and there are things which you must stop and ponder. Either way, the wise man will carefully consider every situation before he acts. He must control his impulses and emotions, and only act after rationally considering what the best course of action may be.

Determine to live your life more seriously than the average person. Don't leave things up to chance any more than you must. Leave the gambling inside the casinos. Live your life with purpose and commitment, or as Musashi put it, live by choice, not by chance.

I choose to live by choice, not by chance.
Miyamoto Musashi

Principle 4
Think lightly of yourself and deeply of the world.

Some people may question whether Musashi actually lived by this principle, as he traveled from place-to-place fighting duels. And if you only looked at that one aspect of his life, I could see how you might think that. But what you must realize when discussing Miyamoto Musashi is that all his duels were fought before he turned 30 years of age. Musashi lived to the age of 63, and like most men, Musashi grew wiser with age.

The *Dokkodo* was written in 1645 one week before Musashi passed away. On that day, he passed *The Book of Five Rings*, or the *Gorin-no-sho*, which was written two years prior, to his favorite student, Terao Magonojo. So, Musashi was over the age of 60 when he wrote both *The Book of Five Rings* and the *Dokkodo*, which means that he had much more wisdom than he did when he was traveling around Japan fighting life-or-death duels with other martial artists.

When one thinks lightly of himself, it means that he is more humble and less prideful. Most men are more foolhardy and have a larger ego when they are younger than after they have had several decades of life experience under their belt. We can safely assume that this applies to Musashi as well.

Moreover, Musashi did indeed gain more wisdom and was more humble when he wrote *The Book of Five Rings* and the *Dokkodo*. Most people do not know it, but Musashi actually wrote six manuscripts, beginning with *Mirror on the Way of Combat* when he was only 22 years old.

His other manuscripts were *Notes on Combat Strategy*, *Combat Strategy in 35 Articles*, and *The Five-Direction Sword Pathways*, along with *The Book of Five Rings* and the *Dokkodo*. If you read each one of these texts in the order in which they were written, you can clearly see a change in Musashi's writing, philosophy, and style.

In the fourth principle, Musashi is pointing out the importance of being humble and not taking yourself so seriously, something which we can assume he learned through his vast experience. People who take themselves too seriously are more nervous, self-conscience, and less confident, although they may appear confident externally. They become more self-absorbed, which skews how they look at the world.

Humility is an important trait for a warrior. A man whose ego is unrestrained will have a hard time viewing other people as being as talented or as good as himself. If a warrior becomes too cocky, he is more likely to be over-confident and underestimate his opponent. It is always dangerous to underestimate any rival or enemy.

In addition, if you haven't developed humility in your life, you will spend more time focused on yourself than on the world. You cannot think deeply of the world when your main focus is always on yourself.

We know that Musashi thought deeply of the world. He started writing his philosophy at the age of 22 and continued to share his teachings up to one week before his death. His focus was mainly on dueling until the age of 30, when he decided to dedicate the rest of his life to studying the greater truths of the world.

Although he never became a pacifist, nor stopped teaching martial arts and the way of the sword, he spent a lot of time alone in intense personal reflection and meditation. He spent many hours in Zazen meditation and even made a pilgrimage to Reigando Cave, where he spent the last years of his life. He became a painter and a poet and took part in poetry gatherings with the most elite men in his region.

Musashi's personal reflection and interest in art and poetry led him to the conclusion that those who have dedicated their lives to such pursuits were on the same level as the samurai as far as their dedication to their personal pursuits. He saw value in the different aspects of the world and not only in the way of the sword.

Those who are single-minded when it comes to what they enjoy sometimes do not appreciate the other aspects the world has to offer. They become more focused on themselves and tend to have tunnel vision as far as the world is concerned, seeing everything through their own limited beliefs.

In this principle, Musashi is urging us to do the opposite of that and think deeply of the world and become more humble. When someone is self-absorbed, he is likely to have poor judgment when it comes to the world. He is more likely to study only the subjects that are important to him at the moment, and disregard, or become indifferent to, the other amazing things that the world has to offer.

Musashi is urging us to become more balanced and to control our ego. Once you start thinking more deeply of the world around you, it opens your eyes to the beauty and artistry that you may have overlooked while your focus was on yourself and your own narrow interests.

As you become more humble, you develop more empathy and understanding of the world. You begin to expand your horizons and start to include other interests in your life. The world becomes a more beautiful place with so much to explore and enjoy.

When you are too self-absorbed, you are constantly concerned about how you appear to other people and what their opinions are; and you become less aware of who you truly are as a person. You tend to not notice all the beauty that the world has to offer. You forget what's truly important in life, as your sole focus is on the image you portray to others and your own personal desires.

Your ego takes control of every area of your life, and you give little to no thought to other people, other than what they think of you. You become overly selfish and self-absorbed. Almost all your actions are based on ego and centered on what you *perceive* is best for you, but you are deceiving yourself.

As your ego takes control of your life, and your total focus is on maintaining the image that you have created for yourself, it starts to work against you. Although you may act self-confident on the outside, you are losing your true self-confidence, as all your actions are measured according to how well you maintain the illusion of your personal image and your ego.

True self-confidence is living your life your way, without concerning yourself with how others see you. Let your ego disappear and become more modest. Stop thinking only of yourself; start thinking more about the world and those around you. How can you help others? How can you make the world a better place?

Think more deeply of the world and break free of your cocoon. One way to do this is to realize that you are only going to be alive on this earth for a short time. You should learn as much as you can about this world while you are here. Enjoy all the beauty and the magnificence that this world has to offer.

Stop focusing merely on yourself and start focusing more on what you can do to help those around you. Musashi certainly did this. No one writes manuscripts simply so he can read them to himself; Musashi wrote his writings to share his wisdom and skills with others. And now, almost 400 years later, *The Book of Five Rings* is one of the most read texts in the martial arts world.

Musashi took his focus off himself and started focusing on the beauty of the world and what he could teach and leave for his students. He put his ego in check. And because he started thinking more lightly of himself and more deeply of the world, he is now known as a genius, not just as a warrior, but also as an artist for his famous ink paintings. He expanded his life to include viewpoints other than dueling with a sword. This would not have happened if he had not evolved and stopped allowing his ego to control his life.

Once you stop thinking so deeply of yourself and start focusing more on the world around you, you will become calmer and more at peace. You will explore different philosophies and ideas. Stop taking yourself so seriously and you will start to enjoy your life more.

Instead of thinking solely about your own interests and hobbies, start focusing more on other people and places, and explore the world in which you live. You will see a beauty that you have been blind to while you were only focused on yourself and your own interests.

As martial artists, we sometimes have a tendency to be on guard most of the time, always on the alert for potential threats; but as you start to think more lightly of yourself, you will find that you start to relax and enjoy life more than before. This doesn't mean that you will become less aware of the possible threats around you, but that you are aware without it interrupting your inner peace and tranquility, and the beauty of the world around you.

Take control of your ego and stop taking yourself so seriously all the time. Take Musashi's advice and think lightly of yourself and more deeply about the world around you. I promise you will be glad you did.

The true science of martial arts means practicing them in such a way that they will be useful at any time, and to teach them in such a way that they will be useful in all things.
Miyamoto Musashi

Principle 5
Be detached from desire your whole life long.

Many sages have taught that you must be detached from desire to have lasting inner peace. Many of Buddha's lessons centered on being detached from desires. He stated that the root of all suffering is desire, and that those who act with fewer desires are calm, without worry or fear.

Musashi, although he was not a follower of any one religion that we know of, spent many years studying Buddhism and knew the tenants of Buddhism well. He saw the value of being detached from our desires. He went as far as to say, "There is nothing outside of yourself that can ever enable you to get better, stronger, richer, quicker, or smarter. Everything is within. Everything exists. Seek nothing outside of yourself."

This is a powerful statement against desiring things outside of yourself. Musashi had learned that the truly valuable things in life come from inside of you. While we are interpreting Musashi's wisdom, we must also remember that he lived in the late 1500s and early 1600s.

Of course, today, we understand that we have different resources that can aid us in increasing our knowledge and wisdom to improve ourselves. In Musashi's day, he couldn't simply log onto the internet to gain knowledge about a specific topic. While he couldn't improve his life with a keyboard, his teachings on being detached from desire still hold true today.

Being detached from desire does not mean that you don't have any desires; it means that you do not allow those desires to rule your life or to control your mind. This is when your desires start to cause problems in your life. Many people desire things they do not have, and most likely will never have, in their life. And they allow those desires to control their mind.

I will give you an extreme example. Let's say that someone badly desires to win the lottery, so much so that his life revolves around that desire. Each week, he takes a large portion of his paycheck and goes out to buy many lottery tickets. And each week, he allows his desire to get him all excited about his prospects of winning the lottery and becoming a multimillionaire.

Then, predictably, he does not win. All his hopes go up in smoke, along with the hard-earned money that he spent on lottery tickets. The rest of the week, he is upset and disappointed, but still thinks that it is just a matter of time before he wins the lottery and becomes a multimillionaire. So, he begins the process all over again, waiting for his next paycheck so he can buy more lottery tickets.

He remains trapped in this endless cycle of desire and suffering, buying tickets, getting all excited, and then in suffering each week as each ticket is thrown into the trash, along with the money that he wasted. Each week, when his numbers do not come in, he beats himself up mentally for being such a sucker.

But by the time his next payday comes around, he has forgotten about the misery of wasting his money and starts the cycle all over again. He lives in a perpetual cycle of getting excited about his desire to win millions of dollars, and then crashing back down to earth as he loses more money, and with it, his hopes for the week. He lives in a miserable cycle of hope and despair caused by his own uncontrolled desire to win the lottery.

Of course, we would all love to win the lottery, but the normal person does not allow that desire to rule his or her life. While this is an extreme example of how desire causes suffering, you can see how being overly attached to your desires can cause grief and anguish in your life.

Being detached from your desires does not mean that you don't have goals or dreams that you want to accomplish. It simply means that you don't put so much importance on those desires that they rule your mind, causing suffering, stress, and a lack of inner peace.

To have lasting inner peace, you must be detached from your powerful desires. When you crave things you don't have, you create suffering because you start to feel that you are lacking something in your life. This feeling of lack is amplified if you compare your life with the lives of others who may have more than you.

As you see others with material things that you desire, it plants seeds of lack, envy, and jealousy. These emotions create negative energy in your life and distract you from living the life that you should be living.

Instead of allowing desire to control your mind and your life, turn your attention inside. As Musashi taught, "Everything is within... seek nothing outside of yourself."

In my book, *The Art of Inner Peace*, I stated that things must get right on the inside before they can get right on the outside. Once you get your mind straight, you stop allowing desire to control your mind or your actions. You start to be at peace, whether or not your desires actually come to fruition. You enjoy your life in the present moment, with whatever you currently have in your life. And if the other things you desire manifest, that is just icing on the cake.

When you have this attitude towards life, your desires or goals won't cause you to suffer. Your focus will be on the journey, not the destination. You will be at peace whether or not you ever reach your desired destination, because your daily life brings you peace, joy, happiness, and satisfaction.

Desiring something so badly that it is constantly on your mind gives birth to feelings of lack, fear, stress, and robs you of your inner peace. You want that thing so badly, but in the back of your mind, you fear you will never get it. That fear leads to stress and frustration, which leads to mental suffering and disrupts your inner peace.

As you transcend the attachment to that overwhelming desire, it enables you to work towards your goals without that overpowering fear of failure or desire for something that you don't currently have in your life. Again, this does not mean that you give up on your goals or dreams; it simply means that they do not rule your mind. You are in control of your mind, not all those external desires.

The *Bhagavad Gita* states, "Detachment is not that you own nothing, but that nothing owns you." Think about that. When you have an overwhelming desire for something which you do not have in your life, it is controlling you–controlling your mind.

It is fine to desire nice things, but it is not acceptable for that desire to control your thoughts or your life. Work to achieve the things that you want in life, but don't allow those things to be your purpose for living. Don't allow them to own you.

Throughout history, slavery has existed in different parts of the world. We all know that when someone is a slave, he is not free; he is owned and controlled by someone else. We also know that those in slavery suffer dearly. They do not live a blissful life of inner peace.

When you allow your desires to *own* you, you are essentially turning yourself into a slave; you are a slave to your desires.

Remember the guy who so badly desires to win the lottery. He is a slave to his desire. He spends so much of his mental energy and his income on lottery tickets that he is owned by his desire to win the lottery.

When you allow your desire to get to that point, you lose your perspective on life. You are no longer objective. That desire becomes a type of addiction that rules your life. You become like a man running on a treadmill–you run and run, but you don't go anywhere and you don't enjoy the journey.

Instead of being ruled by your desires, be grateful for what you have in your life. Get off the treadmill of desire and the suffering that goes along with it. When you are detached from your desire, you gain a different perspective, not only on your desire, but also on your life. You live life with a different attitude.

Be content with what you have, while at the same time, working to improve your life. Don't waste your life being obsessed with one desire after another. Remember, life is what happens to you while you are making other plans. If you focus too much on your plans or desires, you miss out on actually living your life.

If the man in my example had wisely invested a $100 each week, instead of spending it on lottery tickets, he would have created the wealth that he so badly desired, while enjoying his life without being controlled by his desire. But his desire owned him, and he lived his life with tunnel vision, only being able to see what his desire allowed him to see.

Also, when all is said and done, he has nothing to show for his years of allowing his desire to control his mind and his life, except for an abundance of stress and disappointment. He robbed himself of his inner peace and his enjoyment of life, week after week.

Don't allow anything to own you; stay in control of your own mind and your own life. Be detached from your desires and be content with the life that you have while you work for the life that you want. Enjoy the journey and don't obsess over the destination.

There is nothing outside of yourself that can ever enable you to get better, stronger, richer, quicker, or smarter. Everything is within. Everything exists. Seek nothing outside of yourself.
Miyamoto Musashi

Principle 6
Do not regret what you have done.

It is a completely natural part of human behavior to have some regrets regarding some of your past decisions or actions. Most of us have done things in the past that we wish we had not have done. Some of them probably hurt people we love, and we may have some guilt about what we did.

However, the past cannot be changed. It doesn't matter if we are proud of what we did or if we feel guilty about what we did; what is done, is done. There is no going back and correcting our mistakes or our inappropriate behavior.

Moreover, even if we could go back and change things in our past, we most likely would not want to once we consider that any changes to our past would put us on a completely different path than we are on today.

You would no longer be exactly where you are today or who you are today. If you changed something in your past, you may have never met your spouse, had your children, your career, etc. You would not have the wisdom and knowledge that you currently have. Everything in your life would be different.

Consequently, everything in your past has brought you to where you are today. Everything happens for a reason. Sometimes, it is just because you screwed up or made the wrong decision; other times, it is to teach you a valuable lesson or to provide you with wisdom.

No matter what the reason was, it does not change the fact that what is done is done. The past cannot be changed, whether you like it or not. The best you can do is to accept what is, learn from it, and continue to live your life.

Musashi realized this during his short time on earth. He fought his first duel at the young age of 13. That is very young to have taken a life. One has to believe that there were most likely lots of things that Musashi regretted doing after 60 life-or-death duels. But still he admonished us to not regret what we have done.

There were probably many things he would have regretted if he had allowed himself to wallow in clutches of guilt, regret, and self-doubt. However, he was wise enough to realize that living in guilt and dwelling on regrets offered no benefits to his life. The most he could do was live in the present moment and continue to improve himself.

The same philosophy applies to you today. Living in the past and carrying the burden of guilt and regret will only hinder your present journey. Think of every mistake you have ever made as a rock. If you were required to put each of those rocks (mistakes) in a backpack and carry that pack everywhere you go, that pack would soon become too heavy to carry. The more mistakes you make, the heavier the pack becomes; soon it will hinder you in everything you do.

That is what regret and guilt will do to you. The more you carry all your past mistakes and heartaches around with you, the heavier they become. Yet many people not only continue to carry their regrets around with them throughout their life, but they also frequently take their regrets out of their backpack and spend time reminiscing with them. It is as if they enjoy reminding themselves of all the negative things they regret having done and constantly feeling sad about them.

Musashi is urging us to forgive ourselves for our past mistakes. Stop wasting time by regretting things that you have no power to change. The past is over; it no longer exists anywhere outside of your memory. Forgive yourself and move on, determined to live a better life and to not make the same mistakes again.

The past is the past; it is over and done with. Digging up the same old, worn-out regrets again and again offers no benefit to your life. It doesn't make you feel good about yourself, and it doesn't make your life any better. There is only one benefit associated with regret, and that is to gain wisdom from those past experiences.

Furthermore, once you learn the lesson from your mistakes, you should not visit those regrets ever again. You learned your lesson; now it is time to move on. Spending any more time with that regret is simply wasted time that could be used to improve yourself. Continuing to wallow in regret only brings negative energy into your life. It serves no other purpose other than to make you sad or depressed. So why would you ever allow yourself to do this?

We all make mistakes, especially in our younger years. Many of us don't mature as early as we should, therefore we end up making more mistakes than others. Regret is a seductive deception that traps you in the past and stops you from moving forward with your life.

If you feel guilty about something that you have done, meditate on it, learn from it, and determine that you will never make a mistake like that again. Then be done with it! Refuse to hold on to any deep regrets about it; and don't revisit it ever again.

Many regrets are from our distant past when we were young and stupid. But there is another kind of regret that plagues people as well, and that is the regret of *the outcome* of a designed decision that you made. It may not have necessarily been a stupid mistake, but an action you took while doing the best that you could do.

You may have meditated on it and made the best decision that you could make, but the outcome did not turn out exactly how you planned. You should have no regrets whatsoever over such an action! A man can only do the best that he can do in every situation.

If you did the best that you could do with the knowledge and information you had at the time, that is all anyone can do. You only have control over your thoughts, words, and actions, not the outcome of your actions.

Even if you made all the right decisions, that is no guarantee that things will turn out how you want them to turn out. When you have done your best, there is absolutely no reason to have any regrets over your decisions, your actions, or the resulting outcome.

Do the best that you can to make the right decisions. Once you have decided on the right course of action, do the best that you can, with honor and integrity, and then stand by your decision.

Remember, hindsight is 20/20, but you did not make those decisions after the fact; you made your decisions at the time that it was required of you to act. If you make your decision with honor and the right intentions, that is all that anybody can do. Stand by your decision and close the door on that action!

It is only possible to live with no regrets if you live in the present moment. Dwelling on regret and guilt is living in the past; just as dwelling on fear is living in the future. Both will drain your energy and weaken you. Leave the past in the past and live in the present.

When you make a mistake, do the best you can to fix it, and then move on. If you owe someone an apology for your actions, or for a mistake that you made, apologize for it, do your best to make it right, and continue living your life. Those mistakes are over; revisiting those mistakes time and time again is wasting the precious time that you have left to live your life.

If you embrace your mistakes and make them a learning experience, they will enhance your life and your personal growth. Letting go of your regrets will also reduce your stress and increase your inner peace. Free yourself from the weight of regret and live mindfully in the present moment; and do so with gusto.

Regret keeps you focused on the past instead of on the present. Letting go of your regrets frees you to live a life of inner peace in the present moment and allows you to have a greater appreciation for life. There is no reason to allow past regrets to disrupt your thoughts or your inner peace.

Don't be so hard on yourself; forgive yourself and move on. We all have things we regret. The key is to learn from your mistakes, move past them, and live a better life today. Refuse to allow yourself to think about those regrets ever again.

While you don't control the thoughts or memories which arise in your mind, you do have control over which thoughts you allow to dwell there. If a regret that you have already dealt with appears in your mind, actively refuse to allow it to stay there. Just say to yourself, "No! I am finished with that, and I will not allow myself to think about it anymore." Then actively force yourself to think about something else.

Remember, you are not the same person you were 10, 20, or 30 years ago. You are not even the same person that you were last month or last week. You should be growing and becoming a better person each day!

If you are not the same person you were when those regrets originated, then why would you even consider punishing yourself by dwelling on those regrets today? If you are not the same person you were, then the person who you currently are did not commit those mistakes. Move on!

Free yourself from the past! Refuse to allow guilt or regret to bring a dark cloud of negative energy into your present life. Do not regret what you have done. Deal with it, learn from it, and carry on living your life. Live in the present moment, not in the past!

The purpose of today's training is
to defeat yesterday's understanding.
Miyamoto Musashi

Principle 7
Never be jealous.

Jealousy is a natural emotion, even some animals display jealousy when their owners are giving another person or animal attention. Be that as it may, jealousy is not a constructive emotion. It can ultimately cause you many problems and heartaches.

There is more than one kind of jealousy. You can be jealous of another person giving your spouse or partner too much attention. This starts out as a type of concern or a protective feeling, where you feel the need to protect someone who you consider to be "yours" from the advances of another person.

It could be because someone is giving your spouse or partner too much attention, or it could be because your spouse or partner is giving another person too much attention. Either way, your own insecurities cause the feeling of jealousy, thinking that you might lose your significant other to someone else.

The root of this kind of jealousy is a lack of self-confidence. If you were completely confident in who you are, in your self-worth, and in your relationship, then you would not allow jealousy to bother you. It is when you have thoughts of losing your significant other to someone else and never being able to replace him or her with someone who you would love just as much that jealousy rears its ugly head.

Another cause of this kind of jealousy is linked to your past experiences. If you have experienced a partner cheating on you before, it plants seeds of doubt in your mind about it happening again. After all, you probably never thought about that happening to you before his or her actions blindsided you the first time.

Having that happen to you is a very painful experience which can leave you with major trust issues and a determination to never have it happen to you again. This can lead to you distrusting your new partner, or your old flame, if you decided to forgive him or her and continue with your relationship.

Trust issues can be very hard to overcome, especially if many people throughout your life have screwed you over. You learn quickly that many people in this world cannot be trusted. Even if you have never been cheated on before, when you had other people stab you in the back in the past, it takes a long time to develop trust with another person. This is true even with someone that you are in a relationship with.

Nevertheless, this kind of jealousy still originates from a lack of self-confidence and insecurity. The self-confident man would think that someone else would be crazy to cheat on him. After all, a self-confident man with high self-esteem considers himself to be a catch. And if someone did cheat on him, then he would consider her to have a major flaw that he simply did not see.

While that affair would still be painful for a self-confident man, he would get it over and move on with his life, not letting it hurt his self-confidence or his self-esteem. Someone with less self-confidence or self-esteem might be crushed by being cheated on and vow to never trust anyone again.

The way to combat this type of jealousy is to increase your self-esteem and self-worth. If you have high self-esteem, you will simply see this situation as you made a mistake trusting this individual. You would learn from it and vow to be more prudent in your choice next time.

You would not see the other person's lack of fidelity as a referendum on you, but as his or her own character flaw. It would not affect your self-confidence at all. You would know without a shadow of a doubt that you will be able to find someone better, someone with better character and more integrity.

Whether this kind of jealousy stems from being hurt in the past or being protective of your relationship, it stems from a lack of self-confidence. And it is completely obvious from Musashi's writings that he absolutely did not have a problem with self-confidence. He probably saw jealousy as a weakness, and indeed it is.

Besides this type of jealousy, there is another type that is just as common, if not more so–being envious of someone else. Envy is a feeling of discontent or resentfulness brought about by someone else having possessions, qualities, or desirable attributes that you want but do not have.

For example, you may struggle with your finances, but your neighbor just drove up in his brand-new truck. You might feel jealous that he has it so much better than you. This type of jealousy stems from wanting what someone else has, instead of being content and grateful for the things that you have in your life.

You can be envious of an unlimited number of things; anything that someone else has, that you wish you had, can foster jealousy if your mindset is not right. You can be envious of someone's luck, his looks, his family, his possessions, his wealth, or his skills; this list could go on and on.

The way to combat this type of jealousy is to get your mindset right. Stop comparing yourself to other people! Don't compare your life, your looks, your home, your finances, or your material things to what others have. The truth is, you really don't know what their life is like; all you see is what they *allow* you to see.

All you see is your neighbor drive up in that brand new $100,000 truck. What you don't see may be that his finances are a total wreck. He may be in debt up to his eyeballs. He may have to work 70 hours a week to maintain his lifestyle. His wife may be ready to leave him because he is unable to spend much time with his family. You really do not know what is going on in his life.

Don't be jealous of what someone else has, period. If you want something like what your neighbor has, then go work for it and get it. If your friend has a natural talent for martial arts, is more flexible, or is just a natural athlete, and you want to be more like him, then determine to put in the extra work to increase your skills.

If you want something in life, you can have it. This has been proven time and time again by people who grew up in severe poverty and found a way to educate themselves and to obtain the kind of life that they wanted.

There have even been those who have lived under the yoke of slavery and were so determined to break free of their chains and make something of their life that they became bestselling authors, senators, or scholars. What you want in life is available to you if you have the motivation to do what it takes to get it. Just do some research about how some multimillionaires started off. I promise you that you will find their stories very motivating and inspiring.

You may not be able to do everything that your friend can do, but that shouldn't matter to you. Your concern should be to improve yourself and to be the best that *you* can be, not to be like someone else. You are a unique individual; don't sell yourself short by trying to imitate someone else. Happiness is about being content with your life and what you have, not about competing with someone else or comparing yourself to others.

The only person that you are in competition with is yourself. Determine to continually improve yourself every single day. Your goal should be to be better today than you were yesterday; it should never be to be better than someone else. Be the best that *you* can be, then be content and grateful for who you are and what you have in your life.

When you are grateful for the things in your life, it is hard to be resentful or jealous of what others have. You are walking your own path, not their path. Be content with the blessings in your life and don't trouble yourself with what someone else has or who someone else is. What they have and who they are is none of your business; your focus should be on your life, not their life.

If you would stop focusing on other people and what they have in their lives, and start focusing on all the amazing things that you have in your life, you would never have to deal with jealousy. Start taking inventory of all your blessings and you will find that you are greatly blessed.

Do you have plenty of food, clean water, and a place to live? Do you own an automobile, furniture, and a comfortable bed to sleep on? Do you have clothing, shoes, and a job?

Start paying attention to all the things that you have in your life. When you do, you will realize that you have more than enough to be grateful for in your life. Start being grateful for what you *do* have, instead of being envious or jealous concerning those things that you lack. Do this and you will discover that your jealousy and envy will disappear, and your happiness will increase.

Happiness comes from being content with your condition and what you have in your life. When you are content with your life, you are satisfied with what you have instead of being envious of what you don't have. Contentment is the basis for long-term happiness. Learn to be content in whatever situation in which you find yourself, and you will never be jealous again.

There are millions of people all over the world who would love to have your life and be in your shoes. If you must compare yourself with others, compare your life to the lives of people with no home, no decent clothes, no shoes, no food, or no clean water. Get out of your little bubble and widen your view of the world; this will enable you to see how blessed you truly are. If you do, you will realize that you are much more blessed than you thought.

When you are content with who you are and what you have in your life, you will not be jealous of anyone else. Your focus will be on being grateful for what you have and on helping those who are less fortunate than yourself.

Jealousy is a very destructive emotion. If it is not controlled, it can destroy relationships and friendships, along with your inner peace and happiness.

As I stated in an earlier chapter, the theme of detachment and acceptance are common threads throughout the *Dokkodo*. When you develop a sense of detachment and acceptance, you will find that it is much easier to find happiness and contentment in every situation.

Detachment is the state of being objective and separating yourself from external things. Being objective means that you are not influenced by personal feelings or opinions in considering facts; you see things as they are.

Moreover, when you see things clearly, just as they are, you will understand that your happiness and contentment is not dependent on external things or other people. When you are objective about your life, and the things in your life, you will find it easier to distance your contentment and happiness from other people or material things.

As you distance yourself from external things and other people, you will find it is easier to accept everything just the way it is, as Musashi urged us to do in the first principle. Acceptance is crucial to your contentment and your happiness. If you refuse to accept things as they are, there is no way that you can be content with your life; you will find yourself in a perpetual state of discontent, always wanting things to be different from how they are.

When you learn to accept the things that you cannot change, you will discover that it is much easier to be content with life. And when you are truly content, jealousy will have no place in your life. You won't care what other people have, as you are perfectly happy with your own life.

This attitude of acceptance allows you to trust your spouse or partner because you know you will be fine, even if he or she is not faithful. You will accept whatever they do as their choice, and you will respond in whatever manner you choose.

Being detached and accepting things just as they are, will allow your self-confidence and self-esteem to increase. And as they increase to a higher level in your life, you will find that you will become more content with whatever condition in which you find yourself.

Develop your self-confidence to the point that you don't see yourself as inferior to anyone else, no matter how much money they have or what their position may be. When you have developed your self-esteem to a high level, you will not want to trade places with anyone else, much less be jealous of someone else.

Jealousy signals to other people that you have a flaw in your character and that you have low self-confidence and self-esteem. If you find that you have an issue with jealousy, for whatever reason, determine that you will do what you need to do to increase your self-esteem and self-confidence until jealousy is no longer an issue for you.

Whenever you discover a weakness or flaw in your character, refuse to allow it to continue. Decide what you must do to perfect your character and then do it. Be content with your life, but refuse to be content with any character flaws. Remember, your personal goal should always be to be a better person today than you were yesterday.

Never accept an inferior position to anyone.
Miyamoto Musashi

Principle 8
Never let yourself be saddened by a separation.

If there is one thing that you can count on in life, it is that everything in this physical world is constantly changing and is temporary. Even your physical body has an expiration date. While your spirit will live on, your body will eventually wear out. The same goes for everyone in your life.

At one time or another, you are going to have to deal with the separation from those you love. Either you will leave them, or they will leave you. If they leave first, you will be faced with a decision concerning how you will handle the separation.

We know Musashi was a ronin, a samurai without a master. He roamed Japan, answering to no one except for himself. And yet, even Musashi had students and people in his life that he was close to. Remember, he left *The Book of Five Rings* to his favorite student, Terao Magonojo.

While Musashi did not have a wife or children that we know of, he understood what it means to love his friends and students. Still, he cautioned us to never allow ourselves to be saddened by a separation.

Being sad is a common emotion. Even animals experience sadness when they experience a separation from their owner or another animal that they were close to. We all experience sadness from time to time. Some movies even make us sad.

Following this principle requires a great deal of self-discipline. In my opinion, the only way to live up to this principle is to have total conviction in your spiritual beliefs and what happens after the death of your physical body. I will discuss this topic more when we get to the principle on not fearing death. But even then, you will discover that you have moments of sadness when you lose someone close to you.

To deal with a separation without allowing yourself to be sad, you must be prepared beforehand. It helps to remind yourself that everything on this earth is temporary. Every animal will eventually die. Every plant will eventually die. And every human being will eventually die, and that includes you and those you love. Everyone's life is temporary.

This means that every relationship that you have, both good and bad, is temporary and there is nothing that you, nor anyone else, can do about it. Eventually, you will be separated from everyone you know; that is just the way it is.

Even though most everyone is aware of this fact, we tend to put it out of our mind and rarely, if ever, think about it. Most of us don't think about it because we consider it a sad thought, and meditating on it tends to depress us or make us sad.

Nobody wants to think about losing his or her spouse or best friend. It is not a pleasant thought for us to contemplate, although we will all have to deal with this subject.

It takes someone who is extremely evolved to never be saddened by a separation of a close friend or loved one, because most of us consider it a sad event. No one really wants to lose someone close to him; it even makes us sad to lose our dog or long-time family pet.

Being sad is a human emotion that everyone has at some time in his or her life. I believe what Musashi meant by this principle is that we should not allow ourselves to *remain* sad or depressed over a separation, not that we should never experience the emotion of sadness over the event. We should deal with it and then move on and live our life the best that we can.

Choosing to continually dwell on the departure of your close friend or family member will hinder your personal growth and interfere with your goals. If you have ever been extremely sad or depressed, you know you are not very productive during that time. Some people can barely manage to get dressed and function because they are so sad and depressed. And others must take medication to help them deal with their depression.

In Musashi's case, this would not have been acceptable. After all, if you are the greatest sword master in the country, and you have other swordsmen who want to prove their skills against you, you cannot afford to spend time being depressed or sad for any length of time. Allowing yourself to grieve for very long could cost you your life.

The same principle holds true today for those in the warrior professions. If you lose your partner, or your brother, in the heat of battle, you cannot allow yourself to be saddened by that separation, at least not at that time. You must remain focused on what is going on around you or there would be a good chance that you would join your brother sooner than you would like to. That is just a part of being in a war.

But most of us are not in that situation. We do not live in feudal Japan; and only relatively few of us have had the experience of being in a war or in a life-or-death situation. Still, it is good advice to accept what is inevitable and cannot be changed, as I covered previously.

Once again, we find that the themes of detachment and acceptance are vital skills to live up to the principles of the *Dokkodo*. While it is perfectly normal to be attached to those closest to us, we must mentally be detached to a certain degree in order to successfully deal with a separation, such as death. In addition, we must accept that there is nothing we can do about their death; it is simply a part of life.

When we refuse to accept the way things are, we are avoiding the reality of the situation. Many people deal with traumatic or painful events in their lives by simply refusing to accept them. They put the event out of their mind and do their best to ignore it. But all that does is delay the unavoidable. Eventually, they will have to deal with the reality that their friend or loved one is gone. Refusing to accept things as they are never changes the reality of the situation.

Musashi stated, "Truth is not what you want it to be; it is what it is, and you must bend to its power or live a lie." When someone tries to deal with the pain of separation by simply putting it out of their mind and ignoring what has happened, he or she is temporarily living a lie.

In life, you must accept things as they truly are; living in a fantasy world, or in denial, is not mentally healthy. It is better to deal with the separation of your loved one and then go on living your life, just as he or she would want you to. By accepting what has happened, you will avoid unnecessary suffering and sadness.

One way to avoid a long sadness over the death of a friend or loved one is to determine to honor him or her with how you live your life from that moment forward. Honor your friendship by refusing to become sad every time you think of your friend. Determine that you will remember only the good times, the times that bring a smile to your face when you think about him or her.

You can do the same with a close family member. Refuse to remember any negative times or how sad it is that he is no longer here with you. If you carry good, happy memories of that person in your heart and mind, then instead of being sad and holding back tears whenever you remember him, those memories will put a smile on your face.

Is this easy to do? That depends on each individual. It is easier for some people than it is for others. Everyone is different. We each have a different chemical makeup and varying degrees of emotional control. But we can all get to this point; it will just take some of us a bit longer.

These separations become easier if we continually remind ourselves that all things on this earth must end. Nothing in our physical lives is ever permanent. And of course, this includes every single relationship that you have.

We must determine that we will rule our emotions, instead of allowing our emotions to rule us. By learning to think rationally, instead of emotionally, we can learn to control our emotions; like everything else, it just takes some practice.

We know today that grieving is a part of the healing process from the death of a loved one. Don't strive to never be saddened by a separation, rather work to minimize the time that you spend being sad and grieving. And once you are finished grieving for your loss, then refuse to dwell on those sad thoughts again. Make a pact with yourself to only entertain good memories when it comes to your friend or loved one. After all, you will have a lot more good memories of that person than sad memories.

As we get older, we encounter more and more separations in our life, because our friends and family age along with us. That is just part of the human experience. One thing I have started doing is when a close friend passes away, I sit by the fire, enjoy a glass of fine tequila, and toast my friend as I think about how blessed I have been to have known him and to have had him in my life.

Make it a point to remember all the good times. Too many times, when someone dies, all we think about are sad thoughts about our loss and how we will not see him or her again on this earth. But, as Norman Vincent Peale stated, "Change your thoughts and you change your world."

When you change your internal dialog and start to control your thoughts, you can change how you think about the situation. Learn to control your thoughts and your emotions, and you will come closer to what Musashi is urging us to do in this principle. It is not easy, but like everything else, the more you practice this principle, the easier it will get. And, unfortunately, most of us will have plenty of practice perfecting this principle in our lives, as we lose more of the people we love.

Remind yourself that life truly is short. Even when someone lives to the age of 80 something, that time still goes by faster than you think it will. Just ask someone who is in their 80s and he or she will tell you that it only seems like yesterday when they were young and healthy.

Remind yourself of how fast the years go by and keep that fact fresh in your mind. One way to continually remind yourself about how fast life goes by is to use a countdown timer. I started using one of these a few years back and it is truly eye-opening. You can put in whatever age you want, and it tells you how many days and hours you have before you reach that age.

Twenty years may sound like a long time, but once you convert those years into days, it can be astonishing. When you convert 20 years to days, you find that 20 years is only 7,300 days. With your personal countdown timer, you see just how fast it goes. You can set it and keep it on your favorites bar on your web browser and you start to see just how fast those days disappear. You can also use the countdown timer for other things such as projects, etc. Here is the one that I use: https://www.timeanddate.com/counters/.

You may wonder why anyone would do this, and that is a good question. By using the countdown timer, it reminds you just how fast time goes by and to remember to not waste your precious time. It also reminds you to live life to the fullest in the present moment and not to take your time with friends and family for granted; they won't be here forever.

Remember, we all have our individual paths to travel during this lifetime. We never want to lose a close friend or loved one, but that is not up to us. Constantly remind yourself not to take your time together for granted, as we never know when someone's time on this earth will be finished.

Everyone must accept the fact that we cannot control when we will be confronted with a separation. We must let them go; we have no choice in the matter. The only choice we have is how we will respond to those situations. You can choose to fall apart and be depressed, or to control your mind and emotions and celebrate their life. It's all in how you choose to see their departure and how you choose to discipline your mind.

Start making it a point to remember only the good things about the people you have lost, and you will find that those memories will make you happy instead of sad. Don't you think that this is what your friend or family member would want you to do? If he was still on this earth, what do you think he would say to you about it?

In time, all things work to your advantage
when you pursue them with an open heart.
Miyamoto Musashi

Principle 9
Resentment and complaint are appropriate neither for oneself or others.

Musashi is spot on with his advice in principle number nine. Resentments and complaining do absolutely nothing to help you with whatever situation you are dealing with in your life. The fact is, both resentments and complaining make things much worse for you. This is not my opinion; it is a scientific fact.

Complaining is bad for both your physical and mental health. I will give you just a few facts that may surprise you where complaining is concerned. First, complaining increases your cortisol levels. Cortisol is your stress hormone. The more you complain, the higher your level of cortisol rises. Taking this into consideration, the more you complain about something, the more you are inadvertently stressing yourself out.

Besides adding to your stress, higher levels of cortisol in your body can lead to several health issues. It can cause you to be more susceptible to depression, along with causing high blood pressure, digestive issues, and it even increases your risk of having a heart attack.

It also makes you more likely to continue to have negative thoughts, which continue to add to your stress and cortisol levels. The more that you complain, the more you train your mind to focus on negative thoughts which have a destructive effect on your life. Basically, continually complaining is a vicious cycle of negativity that you voluntarily bring on yourself.

Complaining has been shown to damage your memory by shrinking your hippocampus, the part of your brain responsible for your cognitive function. This also affects your ability to successfully handle stressful situations in your life. And it doesn't take long to cause you problems. Just a few days of complaining and high stress can lead to *long-term* damage to your brain. Also, as if all that is not bad enough, studies have shown that complaining shortens your lifespan.

When you consider all the negative effects of complaining, along with the fact that complaining does absolutely nothing to help you live a better life or deal with whatever challenges you are facing, there is absolutely no reason for you to continue to gripe and complain about any issues or challenges in your life.

Refuse to complain about anything for any reason. There is zero value in complaining, and a lot of downside. Musashi instinctively knew this almost 400 years ago. Teddy Roosevelt put it perfectly when he stated, "Complaining about a problem without proposing a solution is called whining." This is absolutely true! And what warrior goes around whining about the challenges in his life?

Instead of complaining about how things are, decide to take control of your life. If you can do something about the situation, then do it; if you can't do anything about the situation, then find a way to use the situation to your advantage. Complaining, or whining, about your circumstances, or a specific challenge you are dealing with, is simply a waste of time that adds to your problems.

Not only should you refuse to complain about things, but you should also not listen to others complain. The negative energy that comes along with complaining is very contagious. If you are constantly listening to others complain, I can pretty much guarantee that their negativity will affect you. Refuse to complain about anything and refuse to give others an audience when they are complaining. It is just not worth the drain on your time or energy.

Along the same lines, resentment towards others has the same effect on you as complaining. Many people have problems when it comes to letting things go or forgiving others. If someone does them wrong, they will hold on to that injury for years, or even for the rest of their life.

When you consider that the guy who you are resenting has probably long forgotten you or the incident, why would you continue to hold on to an emotion that offers you no advantage, but robs you of your time and energy? The guy who you are resenting has moved on, but because you are still holding on to that resentment; you are allowing him to continue to get the best of you.

Don't get me wrong; I am not saying that you should forget what he did to you. On the contrary, I agree with the old Scottish proverb, "Forgive your enemy, but remember the bastard's name." Many people have a problem with forgiveness simply because they don't understand what true forgiveness is all about.

Forgiving your enemy does not mean that what he did was acceptable, nor does it mean that you are okay with what he did. It doesn't even mean that vengeance is not called for in the situation. What it means is that you are mentally letting go of the pain, anger, and hatred where that incident is concerned. You are setting *yourself* free.

Forgiveness is not for the other person. In fact, most of the time, the person who has done you wrong will not ask for, nor want, your forgiveness. He couldn't care less about you. By you forgiving him, it puts you above him; it makes you a better person than him, and no enemy would ever want that. Forgiveness is for you, not your enemy or the person who has wronged you.

It releases you from the mental baggage and negative energy that comes along with holding on to resentment. Don't forget what he did or what kind of person he is, but don't continue to allow that person to live rent free in your mind either. Forgive him for what he did and then do whatever honor calls for in that specific situation.

Like complaining, holding on to resentment invites negative energy into your mind and your life. If you refuse to let go of your resentments, they can quickly turn into a burning hatred of the other person before you know it.

Emotions such as anger, hatred, and resentment are all negative emotions, which weaken you both mentally and physically; they hinder your ability to think clearly and rationally. Strong negative emotions are not conducive to rational thinking and can cause you to make fatal mistakes when dealing with someone.

You simply cannot afford to allow yourself to resent or hate anyone. When you hate your someone, you are allowing him to continue to hurt you by controlling your thoughts and draining your energy. Essentially, you are giving him a certain amount of power and control over you. You are allowing him to disrupt your sleep, increase your blood pressure, and to decrease your appetite, cause health problems, and disrupt your happiness and inner peace.

Musashi knew this, and he knew he could not afford to allow any of his enemies to muddy his thought process. He stated that if you hold anger towards others (which is what resentment ultimately is), then you give them power or control over you. And in Musashi's case, that could have cost him his life.

When you are dealing with a dangerous enemy, you cannot afford to be thinking irrationally or allow anger to cloud your judgment. You must be at your best, not preoccupied with a personal vendetta or hatred towards him. By holding on to your resentment towards the other person, you are giving him an advantage. You are not thinking rationally because of that overwhelming emotion of resentment or hatred.

Overall, if you are wise, you will rid your life of all complaining and resentments. Refuse to allow either in your life, as they only hurt you and offer no benefit to your life or to whatever situation that you may be dealing with currently.

As Musashi stated, neither resentment nor complaints are appropriate for you. Of course, this doesn't stop many people from holding resentments or from complaining daily. Both resenting others and complaining about life's situations are addictive. It takes someone with a rational mind, and a lot of personal discipline, to rid his or her life of these life-draining, negative habits. If you pay close attention, you will see that another one of the overriding themes throughout the *Dokkodo* is self-discipline.

Is it easy to do? Absolutely not! At least not for most of us. But the more you understand the consequences and energy connected to complaining and holding on to resentments, the more you can understand why you *must* discipline yourself to remove these two undesirable traits from your life.

Instead of complaining about things in your life, determine that you will find solutions that will allow you to change those things and use them to your advantage. Complaining doesn't fix anything; it only wastes your time. Instead of complaining, spent that time brainstorming to find a solution.

There are many things in life that you have no power to change, but if you adjust your attitude and change how you perceive what is happening, you can find a way to use those things to your advantage.

People in today's world waste a lot of time. Just think how much more you could get done if you take the time you spend complaining about the things you dislike, and instead, spend that time figuring out how to use those things to your advantage.

As I mentioned in the last chapter, no matter how long you live, your time on this earth is short. You simply do not have the time to waste on complaining about things that you cannot change. If you could track how much time you spend complaining about the things in your life, you would be amazed how much time you are wasting.

People have gotten into the habit of venting and complaining to their work colleagues, their buddies, and their spouse. This time adds up faster than you think. That is not time well spent.

Complaining also goes against Musashi's first principle–accept everything just the way it is. When you accept things as they are, it frees you to see clearly and to work to change the things that you can change. It liberates you from complaining and holding on to resentments, and fosters personal contentment in your life.

If you are constantly complaining, you are not content with your life or things as they are. If you were content with your life, then there would be no reason to complain, would it? Besides all the other negative aspects of complaining, it fosters discontent in your life, which disrupts your inner peace.

You must be detached from your anger or irritation concerning whatever is happening in your life. Recognize the fact that this event or person has angered you or irritated you, then drop it and focus on a possible solution. As Buddha taught, "Holding on to anger is like grasping a hot coal with the intent of throwing it at someone else; you are the one who gets burned."

This is unwise and unhelpful to your life or to the situation which has upset you. Instead of allowing yourself to vent and complain, think rationally and spend your time wisely. Recognize your anger and frustration, and then deal with them strategically instead of emotionally.

Look at the situation like a game. If you were playing a game of chess and your opponent made a move that completely countered your strategy, you would not get angry or complain about it; you would simply study the board and develop a new strategy to win the game. Yet, when it comes to our life, when something goes wrong, or someone disrupts our plans, we tend to complain or get angry instead of simply adjusting our strategy.

If you see everything in life more like a game, then you would not spend time complaining or holding on to resentments. Instead, you would simply adjust your strategy each time that something goes wrong or someone makes a move that sidetracks your plans.

Think of a football game. Many times, a football team will come out and everything seems to go wrong for them. They are trying their hardest, but they keep making mistakes and allow the other team to get ahead of them by three or four touchdowns. The coaches don't go in at halftime and complain about everything; they go in, accept what has happened, and then make adjustments and change their strategy. In doing so, many times, they overcome the mistakes of the first half and end up winning the game.

On the other hand, if the coaches went in at halftime and simply complained about everything that had happened in the first half, and held resentments towards someone for a cheap shot, etc., they would have wasted their time in the locker room instead of making the necessary strategic adjustments. Do you think this strategy would lead to them coming back and winning the game? Of course not!

Accept things as they are and then develop a strategy to deal with them or change them. Complaining about those things changes nothing and only wastes your time that could be spent developing a strategy to turn the situation around and use it to your advantage.

If you discipline yourself to completely stop complaining and to forgive anyone who crosses you, then you will have a distinct advantage over others. You will free your mind and you will be more level-headed, calm, and rational. You will avoid many mistakes by not allowing the negative emotions of anger, hatred, and resentment to cloud your mind. In addition, you will have a greater sense of inner peace in your life.

Let other people lose sleep over their resentments or anger, as you rest easy. While others constantly complain about everything under the sun, discipline yourself to remain quiet and to focus on solving your personal challenges, instead of whining about them. Take control of your emotions instead of allowing your emotions to control you. Rid yourself completely of resentments and complaints. You will be glad you did!

Control your anger.
If you hold anger towards others,
they have control over you.
Miyamoto Musashi

Principle 10
Do not let yourself be guided by the feeling of lust or love.

At first, you may think that this principle does not make sense. After all, every true warrior will fight to defend what he loves. G. K. Chesterton wrote: "The true warrior fights not because he hates what is in front of him, but because he loves what is behind him."

J.R.R. Tolkien wrote essentially the same thing, but slightly differently, stating, "I do not love the bright sword for its sharpness, nor the arrow for its swiftness, nor the warrior for his glory. I love only that which they defend."

When it comes to the principles in the *Dokkodo*, as I stated before, we must consider them from the time period and the circumstances in which they were written. Musashi lived in a very dangerous time. He fought over 60 life-or-death duels with nothing but his swords, and sometimes with only a bokken, a wooden practice sword.

From his point of view, one could not afford to be guided by the feeling of lust or love; he had to remain focused on his sword skills to successfully stay alive. Being moved by feelings of lust or true love could have cost him his life. As far as we know, Musashi never married and did not have a wife or family.

We live in a completely different world than Musashi did, but we still need to be very careful about allowing ourselves to be *guided* by the feeling of lust or love. Such feelings often confuse many people. They basically set their rational mind aside, and the feelings of lust or love completely dominate their thought processes. You can plainly see how this would be extremely dangerous in Musashi's life.

Regarding this principle, I will discuss lust and love separately, starting with the feeling of lust. You don't have to look far to see the dangers of being guided by feelings of lust. Just think about how many well-known preachers and politicians have ruined their careers and reputations because they allowed feelings of lust to guide their actions.

For those who have not disciplined their mind, feelings of lust can easily dominate their rational thought process. And once they let down their guard, the feelings of lust appear to overwhelm them, causing them to do things which they ordinarily would not do.

They can blame their actions on stress or on the fact that some of them believe that they have become so popular or powerful that they are basically untouchable. But no matter how these people try to justify their actions, it all comes back to a flaw in their character and a lack of integrity, especially for those who have promised fidelity to his or her spouse.

When someone has not developed his honor and integrity to a higher level, the feelings of lust can expose their character flaws and can cost him everything in the process. Think about what we can learn from the story of Samson and Delilah.

Samson was clearly told from an early age that his strength and power depended on his never cutting his hair, drinking alcohol, or shaving his beard. Growing his hair was a visible symbol of his dedication to God, and he grew exceptionally strong because he honored his commitment to God.

It was also forbidden for him to marry anyone from any of the seven nations that inhabited Cannan, including the Philistines. But Samson allowed himself to be guided by the feelings of lust and had an affair with Delilah, a beautiful Philistine woman who was bribed to betray him.

He was warned over and over to stop seeing Delilah, but not only did he not heed those warnings, he became infatuated with her beauty and sexuality. He was totally guided by his feelings of lust and let down his guard, and was betrayed by Delilah.

Samson was known as the greatest warrior of his people, but his unbridled lust caused him to be captured by his enemies, blinded, humiliated, and turned into a lowly slave. This all happened because he set his rational mind, his oath, his principles, and his integrity aside and allowed himself to be guided by the feeling of lust.

Feelings of lust can absolutely cloud your judgment and cause you to take unwise actions. Strong feelings of lust can cause one to stop thinking rationally and basically forget about everything but the desire of the present moment. This can be extremely distracting until that feeling is satisfied. And once the feeling of lust is satisfied, and one's rational mind returns, it is often too late to stop the chain of events which have been set in motion and which can destroy one's life or career.

Many people have sacrificed everything in a moment of strong desire and unbridled lust. It can cost you your reputation, your family, your freedom, your financial well-being, and, in certain situations, even your life. Allowing the feeling of lust to guide your actions is never worth the cost.

Both love and lust can affect one's judgment because they are both extremely powerful emotions and can override one's rational mind. While both can cloud your judgment if you are not careful, there is a difference between the two.

Where lust can completely take over one's mind in the heat of passion, love, when properly managed, can be a strong motivating force. Being guided by love is only a problem when you completely lose your self-control and stop thinking rationally.

Love is such a powerful emotion that it can easily transform into jealousy or anger. This is a common cause of fights in bars. Think about the example in a previous chapter about the couple in a bar, where some guy made a pass at the man's wife. Ordinarily, this situation can easily be diffused by letting him know she is married.

But many guys allow their love for their wife or girlfriend to trigger such strong emotions that their love quickly turns into jealousy and anger in this situation. One could say that they are being guided by love, but, in reality, they are being guided by the emotions of jealousy and anger.

Someone's love for another person can cause him to act irrationally if he is not careful. Being guided by the feeling of love can cause one to think foolishly and become careless, or too trusting. Samson was not thinking rationally when he told Delilah about the secret of his strength, and it cost him everything.

If you are familiar with the story of Samson and Delilah, you will recall that Delilah had been bribed by the Philistines twice before. Both times, she asked Samson about the secret of his strength. Being careful, Samson misled her each time; and both times, Delilah proved Samson's concerns to be spot on. She disclosed Samson's secret to his enemies, who tried to capture him.

Both instances should have been a major red flag for Samson, but his lust, or his love, for Delilah overshadowed his rational mind and common sense. After all, if Delilah tried to have him captured twice before, you would think that Samson would never trust Delilah again, especially with his true secret.

But Delilah played on Samson's heart strings and Samson, being guided by his love for her, let his guard down and told her his secret. In a single moment of weakness, caused by allowing his emotions to guide him instead of his rational mind, Samson lost everything.

If Samson had not told Delilah the secret of his strength, she could never have successfully betrayed him. When you allow yourself to be guided by love or lust, instead of deliberate, rational thought, it can cause you to trust the wrong person. Many men and women have had their lives destroyed by trusting someone they shouldn't have while being guided by love.

On the other hand, love can be a powerful motivator if it is combined with self-control and rational thinking. Many warriors have achieved magnificent feats motivated by their love for their wife, family, or fellow brothers in arms. Some of our most cherished stories or movies are based on a warrior overcoming all obstacles to save or avenge someone he loves.

But there is a difference between being motivated by love and being *guided by the feeling* of love. If you are motivated by love, you can achieve great exploits, but to accomplish those heroic acts, the warrior must be self-controlled, disciplined, and think rationally.

If the warrior is simply guided by love, he would become careless and unwise, as the emotion of love has a way of overpowering one's rational mind. He would act on emotion instead of strategically planning how he would overcome his enemies.

When you look at it like this, love is not the problem. Musashi is warning us not to *act on love alone*, but to act on strategic, rational thought. You should allow your love to be a strong motivator, but it should not be the sole determination of your actions. Be motivated by love, not guided by love!

Whenever we allow our emotions to guide us, whether it is lust, love, anger, hatred, or jealousy, we are at risk of making unwise decisions. And those unwise decisions can cost us dearly!

Love, when combined with anger or jealousy, can be a blinding emotion. It can cause one to lose sight of reality and to set rational thinking aside. Here is an example of something that happened in my life many years ago.

I used to coach a competitive soccer team that my son played on, and had coached several undefeated seasons, but this one season was a challenge. I had a couple of rich kids on the team who felt entitled to play, even if they did not put forth any effort. This attitude had obviously come from the boys' parents, as they exhibited the same attitude.

During the last game of the season, one of those boys was not getting much playing time, and his dad stomped over to sideline and started screaming obscenities when I put the boy in to play. I had had to deal with issues with this father before. He was a rich vice-president of some company and never missed a chance to brag about that fact. He obviously thought more highly of himself than he should have.

As I was busy coaching, my assistant coach walked over to him and asked him to stop yelling and to go back to the other side of the field. He stormed off in a huff, cursing and yelling the whole way, and I heard nothing else from him that day.

On the way home after the game, my wife told me that this obnoxious guy had come over to her and my young son after the game and had cursed out both her and my son, who was only twelve years old. I won't repeat what he said, but the things he said were over-the-top obnoxious and threatening.

As I listened to the story, my anger started growing more and more. I pulled into the driveway and told my wife and son to get out and that I would be back soon, that I was going to have a firm "talk" with this guy. My wife was adamant that I should not go, as she knew I was going to do more than talk, but I quickly drove away, burning rubber as I headed back to the soccer field.

As I drove back to the field, I was becoming more and more angry. I was being guided solely by my love for my wife and son, and my anger over what this guy did, and was ready to give this guy the beat-down of his life. I drove up and asked another parent if they had seen this guy and was told he had already left.

This turned out to be a blessing because my anger had reached a boiling point and would have most likely had made a poor decision. I had allowed myself to be guided by love, which had turned into uncontrolled anger, instead of thinking about the situation rationally. This is a great example of allowing yourself to be guided by the feeling of love, and the feeling of love turning into anger and rage.

Never allow yourself to be guided by the feeling of lust or love. Always control your emotions instead of allowing your emotions to control your mind or your actions. A rational mind considers all angles of a situation; it considers the different options and thinks about the consequences of each action. When you allow the feeling of love to guide you, you are acting on pure emotion, not considering the consequences of your actions.

Think about it. Would it have felt good if I would have found the guy and set him straight in a way that he would have never been able to forget? Absolutely! It can be very satisfying to act on strong emotions until the consequences come around.

If I had found that guy, there was an extremely good chance that things would have come to blows. He was already in an uncontrollable rage, and God knows I was more than ready to forcibly shut his mouth for him as soon as I got to the soccer field. But what would have happened afterwards? Would it have been worth it?

This guy would have most likely called the police and had me arrested for assault and battery, even though he would have been the one to throw the first punch, others would have testified that I came to the field angry, specifically looking for this guy.

I would have probably been arrested and had to deal with the police and a corrupt justice system. The rich guy obviously had the money to hire a high-priced lawyer and sue me, in addition to everything else. The whole incident would have turned into a nightmare for me and my family.

But, being guided by the powerful emotions of love and anger, none of that crossed my mind back then. I was purely focused on not allowing anyone to treat my wife and son the way this obnoxious jerk treated them, and on giving him an "attitude adjustment." I had allowed my emotions to get the best of me.

Never allow yourself to be guided purely by the *feeling* of love or lust. Always think rationally and strategically. Control your emotions instead of allowing your emotions to control you. Endeavor to think strategically instead of emotionally. Never allow yourself to be guided purely by lust or love; never allow emotions to overcome your rational mind.

Get beyond love and grief; exist for the good of man.
Miyamoto Musashi

Principle 11
In all things have no preferences.

Principle 11 may seem strange to some people, especially in today's world, but it makes perfect sense from Musashi's perspective. Musashi is not urging us to not care about anything, but to not become closed-minded or narrow-minded.

When you are narrow-minded, you limit your possibilities, which also limits your options. In addition, it limits your overall understanding of what is happening in your world and causes attachments to certain preferences.

Having preferences limits your experiences. Think about it. If you only prefer one specific restaurant or one specific food, that confines your dining experience to a very limited number of restaurants. For example, if you always prefer to eat hamburgers and French fries, then you would never experience Chinese food, Italian food, Mexican food, etc.

Musashi is telling us to stay open-minded and to not limit ourselves to a small number of opportunities. I am sure that you have heard the old maxim that there is more than one way to skin a cat. That is what Musashi is telling us in this principle. Musashi put it this way, "You must understand that there is more than one path to the top of the mountain."

If you have a specific trail that you always hike to get to the top of the mountain, you will limit yourself to the same scenery and experiences every time that you hike that path. But if you understand that there is more than one path to hike on the mountain, you open your world up to varied experiences and views that you would never have experienced if you only hiked your preferred path.

For example, I live outside of Rocky Mountain National Park, and I enjoy taking wildlife and nature photos. Many people come from all over the world to take photos of the elk in the park, and most of them gather in the same spots, taking the same shots of the same elk.

Instead of limiting myself to the photos that I can take from the road, right next to everyone else, I often go off the beaten path and hike deep into the forest. And by doing so, I open myself up to many novel experiences and unique photo opportunities that I would never have had the chance to experience if I had limited myself to the easy preferences that everyone else chooses. I have seen parts of the park that most people have never seen, and I have more unique wildlife photos than they can get sitting on the side of the road.

Now, you could say that hiking through the forest, off the beaten trails, is my preference, and you would be right. But it is actually a preference of not having a specific preference because my trips are always different. No two trips are ever the same; this is what Musashi is trying to get across to us.

The more open-minded you are in life, the more you will experience; and the more you experience, the more knowledge and wisdom you will accumulate. When you always do the same thing, in the same way, you limit your experiences, your wisdom, and your knowledge of the world.

You may think that you *should* prefer one path over another because there is a right way and a wrong way to the top of the mountain. But that is confusing your preference with what it right. When it comes to most things in life, good and bad, easy and hard, or right and wrong, are relative terms. These terms are subjective and change with time, circumstances, and culture.

Many people decide that this is right, and that is wrong. However, they are not talking about universal laws, but simply their own personal preferences. And they absolutely have the right to decide how they want to live their lives. On the other hand, they are limiting their options and experiences in life by doing so.

For example, I know people who believe that dancing is a sin, and that rock music is evil. They are afraid of anything that they have labeled as not a part of their religious beliefs. Therefore, they have missed out on some great music, on many wise philosophies from all over the world; they have limited their enjoyment and their knowledge because of their preferences and their fears.

Many people allow fear to choose their preferences for them; thus, their fears are limiting their experiences. Let's continue with my example of hiking in Rocky Mountain National Park. Many people are fearful of getting lost or of bears, mountain lions, etc., so they stay on the road or only hike well-traveled trails. Therefore, they experience the park like almost everyone else. Although they may enjoy hiking through the forest, they are allowing their fears to choose their preferences for them, missing out on many unique experiences. They play it safe, only allowing themselves to have a small range of experiences in the park.

This principle is not about what you like or what you dislike; we all have certain preferences in life. Musashi is urging us to stop allowing our preferences, fears, or habits to limit our lives, and instead, to be open-minded to varied experiences in our life.

There is also another side to having no preferences, and that is the martial arts side of Musashi's teaching. As you know, Musashi fought over 60 duels with a sword. If he would have had certain preferences as far of how he fought, others could have used that against him to defeat him. It could have cost him his life.

For example, if Musashi preferred only a handful of specific sword techniques, other warriors would have quickly discovered his limited preferences. And, of course, other swordsmen would have trained to find techniques to counter Musashi's preferences.

If you limit your martial arts skills to a small number of techniques or only to fight against specific attacks, your self-defense skills will be limited. Moreover, if you run across someone who has trained in a completely different style, using techniques you are not familiar with, or who understands how to fight dirty, which is the only way to fight in a real fight, your limited self-defense skills would leave you in a dangerous position. Your limited preferences could cost you your life!

Of course, Musashi knew this and taught his students to not develop narrow preferences as they trained. It is much better to understand the universal principles of self-defense and how to take advantage of the human body's weak points. Don't limit your training to only specific memorized blocks, kicks, and punches.

For example, if your instructor always taught you to respond with an upper block when someone throws a straight punch, then that becomes your preferred technique anytime someone throws a straight punch. You are limited to only using an upper block, and a prescribed counter punch, having been taught that *this* is how you respond to *that* specific attack.

But, as anyone who has ever been in a real fight knows, a real fight does not follow any specific rules or prescribed set of attacks and counters. If you prefer only one or two blocks and counters, you have limited your skill set. What happens when an attacker does something unexpected? You're in trouble!

If, instead, you have an overall *understanding* of human anatomy and the actual principles of self-defense and martial arts, then you are not limited to specific blocks and counters. It doesn't matter how someone attacks you, you will know how to respond effectively. You will have many options available to you according to what your attacker does.

Although this may sound like common sense to most people, I have seen many martial artists who develop certain preferences in their training, and they mostly practice the techniques they prefer. There is some value in becoming extremely skilled in a few techniques. The problem comes when someone trains *exclusively* in the techniques that he prefers and starts neglecting those techniques which he does not like, or which are a struggle for him.

Musashi taught that we should be unpredictable. Therefore, you should not have any specific preferences or patterns in your life. If you do the same things, in the same way, each day, you become very predictable.

I just saw a documentary on hitmen and the reporter interviewed several hitmen with their faces covered and voice changed. Each one of them stated that they watch their target for a specific amount of time to discover their preferences and habits. After that, killing their target was very easy, as their preferences made them predictable.

Most preferences are simply habits that people do without giving their actions much thought. They prefer to stay in their comfort zone instead of trying anything new or out of the ordinary. Consequently, they become boring and predictable; they rarely deviate from their pattern. This limits their knowledge and their experiences and makes them extremely predictable.

Be open-minded and unpredictable; don't limit yourself. This is a big world, and you are only here for a short time; experience as much of it as you possibly can. Don't be afraid to get out of your comfort zone. Try new things and enjoy new experiences. Learn as much as you can and gain valuable knowledge and wisdom. In all things, have no set preferences, but be open-minded and enjoy your life as it unfolds.

You must understand that there is more
than one path to the top of the mountain.
Miyamoto Musashi

Principle 12
Be indifferent to where you live.

When it comes to the wisdom and practices passed down to us throughout the ages, as I have already made clear, we must always consider what was written in the context of the time and culture in which the author lived. The world is constantly changing. Along with it are changes in people's attitudes, cultural beliefs, and morals, and how people need to live to strive and be successful in their current era. This certainly applies to the wisdom of Musashi.

So, when it comes to Principle 12 of the *Dokkodo*, we must not only think in terms of how Musashi's wisdom applies to us today, but also in terms of how the culture was during his time and how he lived his life. Musashi was a ronin, a wandering samurai who had no lord or master and who had severed all links to his family or clan. He wandered from place to place, fighting duels and proving his skills against other warriors, finally ending up living in Reigando cave.

Reigando cave literally means Spirit Rock Cave and lies to the west of Kumamoto, Japan. It became Musashi's home after years of moving from place to place. This is where Musashi spent the last two years of his life and where he wrote both *The Book of Five Rings* and the *Dokkodo*, as I mentioned earlier.

He obviously was not particular about where he lived or about acquiring many personal possessions or a family. Musashi lived his life for himself, teaching his students martial arts, and writing his various manuscripts, where he passed on his wisdom for future generations. You can plainly see where he might write this principle for others, as that was how he lived his life.

On the other hand, for most of us in today's world, we must be concerned about where we live. Our modern world has dangers that Musashi could not have envisioned. If someone threatens us with a weapon today, it is not acceptable to rid him of his head and simply go on living our life as if nothing had happened; doing so would cost us dearly. In addition, we are not ronins. Most of us have families to support and other responsibilities.

So, what wisdom can we take from this principle? To start with, we can think about how Musashi moved from place to place but maintained his true character and his values. Wherever he was, he was living in the moment, happy and content with his life. His happiness did not depend on material possessions or other people. Wherever he laid his head was his home, and he cultivated his inner strength and inner peace wherever he found himself.

Likewise, your happiness does not depend on where you live; you can be happy no matter where you live in our world. Happiness is something that comes from inside you; it is not dependent on external things, but rather your inner attitude and perspective. Obviously, Musashi was happy even living in a cave. But not everyone wants to live in a cave; we do have a preference concerning where we live.

Since your happiness comes from within, you can take it with you wherever you go, just like Musashi did. It does not matter if you live in a big, fancy house or if you live like a mountain man; you can still be happy and content.

Additionally, if you are sad, depressed, frustrated, or angry, these feelings do not simply disappear because you move somewhere new. Just like your happiness, these feelings come from within, and you take them with you wherever you go. Your happiness, and your discontent, come from your perspective, how you look at life, and are controlled solely by your thoughts, not by your surroundings.

My Grandfather used to tell me a story of two people who moved to a new town and an old man who they approached for information. The first guy came up to the old man and said, "I just moved here. What are the people like?"

The old man responded, "Well, what were the people like where you lived before?"

The man said, "Oh my gosh! They were terribly unfriendly, snobby, rude, and just overall, not very nice people."

The old man said, "Yeah, that is what you will find here as well." And the guy walked away feeling sad and disappointed.

A couple of days later, another man, who had just moved his family to the town, met the same old man. The guy said, "We just moved here. What are the people like in this town?"

Again, the old man responded with a question, "Well, what were the people like where you came from?"

The man responded happily, "Oh, they were really nice people! We hated to leave our community, but my job required that I move my family here. We just loved the people there very much and are really going to miss them."

The old man said, "Well, that is exactly the kind of people you will find here." And the man left happy with a big smile on his face.

So, what's the point of this story? Wherever you go, you take your attitude and your problems with you. You can't escape your problems or a poor attitude by moving to a new place. If you have internal issues, those must be addressed internally; nothing externally will change them.

Also, your attitude, expectations, and perspective color your world. If you expect people to be rude, hateful, untrustworthy, and unfriendly, that is exactly the kind of people you will find. If you expect people to be kind, helpful, friendly, and loving, those are the kind of people you will find.

It is not the place you live in, but your expectations, attitude, and perspective that matter, and you take those things with you wherever you go. Your thoughts attract those things which you think about into your life. What you give your attention to increases.

In my younger years, it seemed like I got screwed over a lot; and it wasn't just from strangers, but from good friends or people I knew. I allowed those occasions to affect my expectations of other people. And I always had my guard up and expected people to lie, cheat, steal, and take advantage of me as much as they could.

And what did I attract in my life? I attracted exactly those kinds of people. It seemed repeatedly, I somehow met people who were untrustworthy, disloyal, and who stabbed me in the back. I attracted those kinds of people because I *expected* people to be that way, and many were. Each time someone screwed me over, in my mind, it confirmed my beliefs about people.

You attract into your life those things which you give sustained thought to. If you believe that most people are bad and will take advantage of you, you will find more of those kinds of people. If you believe that most people are kind, helpful, and good people, you attract more of those kinds of people into your life. I know this may seem weird to you, but it is true.

From what we know, Musashi was not really a people person; he wandered from place to place and was always on the move for the most part. Because of his lifestyle, he most likely had very little as far as luxuries or possessions. Those things were not important to him; what was important was maintaining his martial art skills, his conduct, and his values.

Today, those with character, honor, and integrity still place great importance on their conduct and values. That doesn't change according to where you live. You take your honor and integrity with you, no matter where you live or where you go.

Also, consider the fact that during Musashi's time, most people lived without most of the luxuries that we have today. This is especially true of a ronin. During that time, the samurai only had the wealth that his daimyo (feudal lord) allowed them to have or gave to them. This could also be taken away from them, as could their life, as the daimyo pleased. He could demand that a samurai commit seppuku (ritual suicide) at any time he pleased.

Considering these facts, it is easy to see why Musashi placed little importance on where he lived. He was not in the service of any daimyo and only answered to himself. He was free from the control of anyone else, and that was more important to him than a home or material possessions.

We live in a totally different world today, but we can still learn from Musashi's wisdom. A house, land, and material possessions can be taken away from you; your real wealth in this world is your health, your principles, your wisdom, and your honor. No one can take your knowledge, wisdom, honor, integrity, or happiness from you. You have total control of those things no matter where you live or what material possessions you have, or you lack.

While it is wise to locate your family in a desirable and safe place, you must realize that there is no right or wrong place to live, just as there is no right or wrong way to live your life. I am not referring to morals here, but rather living your life your way.

Have a certain amount of detachment concerning where you live; don't be overly attached to a place or home. Be flexible about the changes that life has in store for you. If you maintain your inner peace and contentment, and live in a fairly safe place, you can be indifferent about where you live. The place is not as important as your attitude, perspective, and inner peace.

If you know the Way broadly, you will see it in everything...
The approach to combat and everyday life should be the same.
Miyamoto Musashi

Principle 13
Do not pursue the taste of good food.

At first, principle 13 appears to be a form of self-denial by denying yourself the pleasure of good food. Of course, everyone enjoys the taste of good food. After all, do you prefer your favorite meal cooked to perfection with the perfect amount of seasoning, or do you prefer food which is tasteless and bland? We all enjoy food which is well prepared and tastes good.

In principle 13, Musashi is not suggesting that we not enjoy our food or that we deny ourselves the pleasure of a well-prepared meal. He did not say that we should not *enjoy* the taste of good food; he said that we should not *pursue* the taste of good food.

When you pursue something, you have a passion for it; you strive for it and devote yourself to it. It can become an obsession for you if you are not careful. Musashi's passion was the art of the sword and martial arts; he was not pursuing fine food.

I am sure that Musashi saw people who had a passion for the taste of good food during his travels. He probably noticed that they were overweight and out of shape. They most likely spent more time eating and little to no time exercising or training their body. And he most likely noticed how easy it would be to defeat these people in martial arts combat.

So, his admonition to not pursue the taste of good food is wise. I am sure that Musashi enjoyed well-prepared food as much as the next man did, but food was not his passion. He was most likely just as satisfied with a plain meal as he was with a delicacy, and maybe even more so since he probably looked at food as fuel for his body and was not particular when it came to what he ate.

What he is warning us against is being *obsessed* with the taste of good food and pursuing it as a goal or passion. If you are obsessed with the taste of good food or expensive, choice food, then you may not be getting the right nutrition for your body. In addition, you would spend a great deal of your income on food, which might not offer you the nutritional value that your body needs.

We do not have any real historical information about Musashi's financial situation, but it is safe to say that after he became a ronin, he did not have as much wealth as he did as a samurai who was being paid to serve his daimyo, which is the way Musashi grew up as a male in a samurai family. Once a samurai was no longer in service to his lord, he was no longer receiving any income or a home from him. He was on his own.

Moreover, we can assume that the best tasting food during the 16th and 17th centuries was not only more expensive, but was probably not as easy to find as he traveled. As a ronin, Musashi most likely made a living by teaching his martial arts skills to others. Unless he was honored by a student, or someone else on his journeys, he most likely ate off the land, mainly fish with vegetables or rice, which was the staple diet in Japan, and still is in many places.

Of course, we do not have that kind of information about Musashi; I am merely assuming that his meals were much like those people in Japan who did not have riches. Either way, it doesn't change the fact that he is not telling us not to enjoy good food, but not to pursue it. Those are two different things entirely.

As I stated, we can assume that Musashi saw food as merely fuel that he needed for his body to continue training and to live. Today, we know much more about nutrition and what we should and should not put into our body. People did not really have that kind of information in the 16th and 17th centuries; they mostly knew whether they had plenty of food or were going hungry.

Today, we understand much more about nutrition and what our body actually needs. We also know that a lot of the food that our taste buds desire is not actually healthy for us. I will not get into how bad sugar or refined foods are for you, as that is not the topic of this book. But most of us realize delicious desserts are not foods that are the best choice to fuel our body or to build muscle. Pursuing those kinds of foods will lead to obesity and health problems.

That does not mean that we cannot enjoy those foods in moderation. Moderation is the key. I believe that is what Musashi is telling us in this principle. We should not allow ourselves to be addicted to anything, whether it is food, sugar, alcohol, or drugs. Many people do not realize that sugar is just as additive, and even more so, than many drugs.

Overall, this is great advice for our current culture. You can go into any restaurant, in any town or city, and you will most likely witness many people who are overweight and out of shape, sitting there with a plate of food large enough for two or three people. Obesity is an increasing problem in the Western world.

It has become such a problem in our society that drug companies are now making billions of dollars by developing weight loss drugs. The weight loss industry is a multi-billion-dollar industry. It includes workout books, videos, diets, and, of course, the drug industry. This is a sad state, especially since most of the people who have issues with their weight have caused their problems themselves by pursuing the taste of good food, or to be more exact, the addictive taste of junk food and prepackaged foods.

Much of the food that is causing the overweight epidemic has very little nutritional value. That being said, you can overeat no matter what kind of foods you are eating, but the vast majority of the weight problems in the world come from eating foods that offer very little nutritional value.

Warriors and athletes understand that what you put in your body matters. You cannot perform at your optimal level if you are eating junk and not getting the right amount of protein and foods with good nutritional values.

As this principle states, the primary focus of your diet should not be for taste or the gratification of your senses, but to fuel your body and maintain good health. That will never change. In our society, most people have a wide selection of food. But it is safe to say that most of the people reading this choose their food according to what they are in the mood for on any given day. And there is nothing wrong with that if you are making wise choices.

The problem starts when you begin to choose your meals solely on their taste instead of choosing food that is healthy and nutritional. If you are choosing your food merely on what you are in the mood for, or exclusively according to your desires or taste, then you are most likely not eating as healthily as you should. You are pursuing the *taste of good food*, instead of choosing food that is *good for you*.

Eating healthy food that fuels your body does not have to be bland or tasteless. There are many cookbooks on the market that show you how to choose and cook healthy foods that also taste good. Even most of the restaurants that you go to today have options on the menu that are healthier for you.

The problem is not a lack of nutritional food, or too many choices, but rather a lack of personal discipline. It does not matter how many healthy choices the grocery stores or the restaurants have if you lack the discipline to choose them and decide to choose food which is not good for you instead. That is pursuing the *taste* of good food instead of pursuing nutritional food that is good for you.

If we look at it like that, what Musashi is telling us is to take charge of our desires and develop self-discipline. There's that pesky self-discipline term again. As most of you know, it takes self-discipline, and sometimes a lot of self-discipline, to make a healthy decision when it comes to our food choices. Many people hate the term "self-discipline," as it puts the responsibility on them instead of some external issue they can blame for their problems.

We are used to eating whatever we are in the mood for on any given day. Is that not pursuing the taste of good food? Is choosing a piece of cake or pie for a snack, instead of some nuts or fruit, not the same thing as pursuing the taste of good food? Of course it is! And we all know which of those choices is better for us.

At first glance, some of Musashi's *21 Principles* seem odd to us or they seem like they do not apply to our modern world. You must stop and think about them from a different angle. As I said, there is a big difference between not *enjoying* the taste of good food and not *pursuing* the taste of good food.

When we read the *Dokkodo*, we must go beyond how the principle initially seems and start to think about the subtle meaning behind each principle. Some of the principles are straightforward, and some of them you must think about for a while.

By all means, enjoy the taste of good food, but don't become *obsessed* with the taste of good food. Don't allow any food, or anything else, to control your actions or your life. Have the self-discipline to choose most of your food according to its nutritional value instead of only according to your taste buds.

As with many things in our life, moderation and self-discipline are the difference between something becoming a problem or something being completely acceptable. Be mindful and disciplined when it comes to your food. Too much indulgence, or a lack of self-discipline, can lead to health issues and sidetrack your goals.

Today is victory over yourself of yesterday;
tomorrow is your victory over lesser men.
Miyamoto Musashi

Principle 14
Do not hold on to possessions you no longer need.

This principle was obviously not an issue for Musashi. As a wanderer, he only kept the possessions that he could carry with him. He did not have a house, the need for furniture, a bed, or decorations. The only possessions that he apparently had were whatever could travel with him on his journeys. If it was something that he did not need, he got rid of it.

Most of us today are in a completely different situation. Even most of us who do not own a home have a place that we call home, either an apartment, a room, or a rental home. Therefore, it is much easier for us to fall into the trap of holding on to possessions long after we need them or have a use for them.

Some of us hold on to possessions thinking that we may need them later, so we store them. Others simply cannot seem to let anything go, even if they mentally know that they will not need the item again. Still, others may know that they have no use for a certain item, but they have an emotional attachment to it, so they keep it indefinitely.

The attachment to possessions is limiting for us. The more possessions we have, the more we are anchored to where we are. Think about it. If you are like me, when I was young, I could pack all my possessions and move on the spur of a moment. Moving was fairly easy. But now that I am older and have accumulated more stuff, moving would be a nightmare. I would actually have to hire movers to move to a new place.

The more that you are anchored by your possessions, the less likely you are to be spontaneous or to move to a different place. It is simply too much of a hassle and you get comfortable with your current lifestyle.

Musashi is telling us not to get too attached to our material possessions. If something no longer serves a purpose or benefits you in some way, why not sell it or give it to someone who actually needs it? Part with unneeded possessions freely and with a giving heart.

When you give something to someone who really needs it and appreciates it, that possession makes you much happier than if you just store it away in a closet, or in your attic, and don't see it or think about it for months or years. Giving to others will increase your happiness and you will feel better about yourself. And, if you are honest, you most likely would not miss the item that you are giving away.

Happiness does not come from possessions. If you travel the world, you will find people who have almost nothing, but who are much happier than many people who have an abundance of everything they could possibly want. Having fewer possessions makes many people happier because they have less to deal with and less to worry about. Living a simple life is often less stressful than living life in a large home, packed with valuable possessions.

People see a beautiful house with a pool, manicured lawn, etcetera, and think about how nice it would be to have a place like that. But what they don't see is how expensive the mortgage and insurance are. They don't see how much money it takes to maintain a large house with all those extras, or how much it costs to simply buy the furnishings for that home. And they don't see the stress it can put on someone to maintain that lifestyle.

The more that you have, the more you must deal with, whether it is in repairs, maintenance, taxes, updates, etc. Also, when you have a really nice place like that, you tie yourself down to the rat race, constantly being required to continue to work to pay those bills. Many people are stuck in a job which they hate because they simply cannot afford to quit and follow their passion. This adds to their overall stress level, but not really their happiness.

You don't need a lot of things to make you happy; happiness comes from inside you. You can be just as happy with very little as you are with an abundance of possessions. Being happy is totally up to you and has very little to do with anything externally.

In addition, once you start to accumulate more and more possessions, your home begins to feel cluttered and disorganized, which can also add to your stress. While it may sound strange, material things can become a burden for many people. This could be the reason that we are seeing a booming industry with people buying tiny homes, instead of the larger, traditional houses.

Those who elect to live in those tiny homes have very little choice as far as having a lot of belongings; they have nowhere to store them or to keep them. They are basically forcing themselves to live a simpler, uncluttered life. Although those tiny homes are not for me, many people seem to enjoy that lifestyle.

The bottom line is we should not become overly attached to most of our material belongings. You only own those things for a short period of time; they are not your permanent possessions. You can't take them with you when you die. They are simply temporary possessions for you to enjoy and use while you are on this earth. If something is not useful, why continue to hold on to it when there may be someone else who would love to have it or who needs it?

Musashi did not have to make those kinds of decisions because, as far as we know, he had no place to store or keep a lot of possessions. He kept what he needed and took those possessions wherever he roamed.

That being said, there are possessions that are wise to keep for later use. The wise man stays prepared for unseen circumstances. You may not use your pry bar every day or even every year, but it is very nice to have it when you need it, instead of getting rid of it and then having to buy a new one each time you need one.

There are many possessions that fall under this category. Think about preppers for example. Do they actually need all the food, water, and other things that they store up? Not at the present moment. But their goal is to stock up in order to be prepared for emergency situations. This is an example of being prepared. It is kind of like an insurance policy.

This is not what Musashi is referring to. Again, you must study his principles closely. He did not say do not hold on to many possessions, but rather, do not hold on to possessions *you no longer need.* Few of us are wanderers today. We have homes and lives that require us to have a certain number of possessions.

For example, you may not use your hammer or other tools frequently, but they certainly are nice to have when you need them. It would be a waste of money and unwise to buy a hammer and a screwdriver every single time you need one. Most of our possessions fall into this category.

At the same time, most of us have possessions that we have stored that, not only do we no longer need them, but we probably have forgotten about them. They are just there, cluttering your home, your closets, or your attic. These are the type of material possessions that Musashi is referring to. They are no longer needed, so don't hold on to them. Sell them, donate them, or give them to someone who needs them.

By getting rid of the things that we no longer need or use, it gives us a greater appreciation of the things which we do have. In addition, decluttering your home makes your home feel cleaner, more organized, and gives you a greater feeling of inner peace and tranquility.

Furthermore, it is a good practice to help those in need. There are many people in this world who lack things which most of us take for granted. If you have too many pots and pans, share some with those who do not have enough. If you have clothes that you have not worn in over a year, donate them. There are many people who can't afford new clothes and who would feel blessed to have them.

There is not much that feels better than helping those in need. When you have possessions that are not being used, and which you most likely will never use again, why keep them? By giving them to those in need, you are not only helping those people, but you are decluttering your home as well. It is a win-win situation!

It feels good to declutter your home; it makes you feel more in control of your life and more organized. And it adds to your inner peace, not to mention it saves you hours of stress, looking for something that you cannot find in the clutter of your home.

The *Book of Proverbs* tells us, "Whoever is kind to the poor lends to the Lord, and he will reward them for what they have done." And the *Bible* states, "Anyone who has two shirts should share with the one who has none, and anyone who has food should do the same." A good man is always willing to help those who are less fortunate.

Keep what you need, or what you will need later, and get rid of what is no longer useful to you. Donate those things you don't use to those in need and help those who are not as well off as yourself. Remember, by being a blessing to others, you inadvertently attract blessings to yourself. It is wise to continually make deposits in your karma account; you will be glad you did.

It may seem difficult at first, but everything is difficult at first.
Miyamoto Musashi

Principle 15
Do not act following customary beliefs.

In this principle, Musashi is telling us not to decide upon our actions simply because of popular customs or beliefs, or because of what the majority believes, or how they act. This is something that you should absolutely take to heart!

Sages throughout the ages have taught that you should think for yourself and not let others think for you. When you follow the crowd, or follow old, worn-out traditions and beliefs simply because that is how it has always been done, you are not thinking for yourself. You are simply allowing others to do your thinking for you.

The Chinese prince and philosopher, Han Fei Tzu, put it this way: "The reason you cannot rely upon the wisdom of the people is that they have the minds of little children." If you pay close attention to what the majority of people are doing, you will find that most of those people are not people which you would go to for advice. Be careful who you trust to give you advice!

The 18th century philosopher and writer, Johann Wolfgang von Goethe, also warned us about following the wisdom of the majority. He put it this way: "Nothing is more disagreeable than a majority; for it consists of a few powerful people in the lead, rogues who are adaptable, weak people who assimilate with the rest, and the crowd that trundles along behind without the slightest notion of what it's after."

Those who think for themselves and are observant know that it is unwise to always follow customary beliefs or to follow the crowd. The crowd, or the majority, are generally not made up of upstanding, thoughtful people. Most people simply do what they see others doing, or they follow the customs which their parents and grandparents taught them.

Musashi is urging us to think for ourselves instead of just following what everyone else does. If you look at Musashi's life, it is obvious that he followed his own set of rules. Many samurai during that time considered Musashi to be a rogue because he did not follow samurai traditions when it came to his duels. But this did not faze Musashi; he thought for himself and lived by his own rules.

Musashi would do things to purposely irritate or offend his opponents. He would show up late or show up much earlier to determine how he could use the geography to his advantage. Musashi used whatever he could to be victorious. He would throw dirt in his opponent's face, stab at his face, make sure the sun was in his opponent's eyes, or insult him repeatedly to anger him.

He knew that if he could anger his opponent, he would have an advantage. What others thought about him, or his tactics, did not matter to Musashi; what mattered was walking away victorious and living to fight another day.

This was a type of psychological warfare, and Musashi was an expert in what the other samurai considered fighting dirty. Musashi sought to psychologically destroy his opponent's mind first and foremost, then destroying his enemies physically was a given.

While Musashi had mastered the rules of different fighting styles, he thought for himself and broke the rules as he pleased, bewildering the other samurai who were strict followers of tradition and believed in fighting with honor, instead of fighting to win. He threw the tradition-based rules of dueling away, and by doing so, he not only angered and bewildered his opponents, but won every single fight.

Musashi stated, "Your attitude should be superior to that of others. You can conquer by virtue of your own mind." This is the attitude of someone who refuses to follow traditional beliefs or to blindly follow the crowd. If your attitude is superior to most others, you will absolutely think for yourself, as you won't have much confidence in the wisdom of the crowd or in following long-held traditions. This was Musashi's attitude.

It was almost like Musashi thrived on being different from everyone else. It is said that he never bathed or brushed his hair, which some say was so long that it hung down to his waist. He refused to wear his hair in the fashion of other samurai and obviously refused to live the lifestyle of the samurai.

In this principle, he is teaching us to think for ourselves, not to blindly follow what others believe to be the truth. We should search for, and discover, the truth for ourselves. Don't just believe something because someone else declares that it is true. He is urging us to form our own opinions and beliefs about the world in which we live, instead of depending on others to do the thinking for us.

Musashi was obviously an independent thinker with the self-confidence to live by his own beliefs. He was willing to challenge the traditional norms of the time, and it served him well. He knew that just because everyone else was doing something in a specific way, that did not mean it was necessary or that it was even the best way to act. Moreover, just because no one else does something, that is not evidence that it is a bad idea or that it should not be done. You must decide for yourself what is best for you.

Buddha basically taught the same philosophy, stating, "Do not believe in anything simply because you have heard it. Do not believe in anything simply because it is spoken and rumored by men. Do not believe in anything simply because it is found written in your religious books. Do not believe in anything merely on the authority of your teachers and elders. Do not believe in traditions because they have been handed down for many generations. But after observation and analysis, when you find that anything agrees with reason and is conducive to the good and benefit of one and all, then accept it and live up to it."

Think for yourself and determine your own path. Do your own thing and decide how you will live; don't let others decide for you. God did not put you on this earth to be just like everyone else. If that was what God wanted, He would not have given everyone their own mind and the ability to reason and think for themselves.

Don't be afraid to challenge the customs and norms of your society. Don't follow the masses, because in doing so, you may discover that you are simply following the asses. Think for yourself instead of being one of the sheep!

In an earlier principle, we found that Musashi encourages us to maintain an open mind and be open to other ideas and other ways of doing things. You must be open to other ideas and beliefs, not so closed-minded that you cannot hear or discuss other philosophies without being fearful of the thoughts of others.

I have studied many different philosophies and religions over the years and have found that you can always find something useful in almost all of them. The key is to take what you feel is useful or true and leave what does not agree with your spirit. If you are living as you should, you will feel whether or not something is right; let your own spirit and reasoning determine what you consider to be true. If you listen to your inner being, it will guide you.

Once you have developed this spirit of independence and self-awareness, you must be on guard against disagreeing with tradition simply because everyone else goes along with it. The fact that the majority believes in something, or follows a certain tradition, is not necessarily evidence that it is wrong. Once you start to think for yourself and go your own way, it is all too easy to just assume that a train of thought must be wrong because all "those people" believe it to be true.

That is not thinking for yourself, but allowing your ego to think for you. Some people just enjoy going against the grain to irritate others or simply to be different. It is not that they have given the issue a lot of thought and decided that they disagree with it, but rather they enjoy being different and standing out from the crowd.

This is not the same thing as not following customary beliefs because they do not agree with your own ideals or independent thought. It is simply allowing your ego to oversee your actions, which is not wise. There is a big difference between thinking for yourself and determining that a tradition or philosophy does not ring true for you, and in just enjoying going against the grain for attention or to simply rub some people the wrong way.

Think for yourself and decide what path you will follow, but make sure you are actually *thinking* and not simply acting. Don't do anything simply because it is the way it has always been done or because it is how you were taught. Always remember, you may have been taught wrong.

In everything, take time to consider the issue and determine what *you believe* about it. Don't believe anything simply because you saw it on the news or someone else said it. Also, you must remember that many traditions have survived the test of time because they *are true*. The use of herbal medicines or traditional Chinese medicine which have been used for over 5,000 years are good examples.

The point is, you need to take the time to think for yourself and do your homework. Don't believe anything just because others believe it. Do your best to get to the underlying truth in all things and have the courage to live your life your way.

The path that leads to truth is littered
with the bodies of the ignorant.
Miyamoto Musashi

Principle 16
Do not collect weapons or practice with weapons beyond what is useful.

This principle is going to hit many martial artists and self-defense practitioners very hard. I know many martial artists who collect swords, knives, and different martial arts weapons and who have a lot of them. The same thing applies to survivalists and self-defense experts. So how does this principle apply in today's world?

First, we must remember once again that Musashi was a wandering ronin who carried all his belongings with him as he traveled. So, it makes perfect sense for his lifestyle. He knew that everything he took with him meant that there was something else that he could not take on his travels.

Musashi could not afford to take every kind of weapon with him; he had to pack efficiently and carefully. Everything that he packed came at an equal cost. Remember, he was not packing a truck, a car, or a camper; he either traveled by horse or on foot. If you have done any backpacking, you realized that a 40-pound pack is about all you want to carry, and even that gets heavy. So, he had no choice about collecting many weapons.

Also, Musashi's weapons of choice were his katana, wakizashi, and probably a tanto, all bladed weapons. There are a variety of martial arts weapons which were used by the samurai, but the samurai also had homes and could afford to have several different weapons, all of which they were proficient in using.

Additionally, that is only the first half of this principle. The second part states that we also should not practice with weapons *beyond what is useful*. This will also be hard for some martial artists to swallow since many practice with weapons that they would most likely never use in a self-defense situation.

Being a martial artist, I am guilty of the first part of this principle myself, but I have always mainly trained for self-defense. I did not train much with a sword or any of the other martial arts weapons simply because I felt I would most likely never need to use one for self-defense. And, on the outside chance I needed to use a sword for self-defense, I figured that I have enough common sense to know that the "pointy end goes in the other guy."

Seriously though, I have always felt that it was more important to learn the art of the stick–the bo, the jo staff, and the hanbo. Makeshift sticks are available in many places, even if you don't have one with you. You can use a mop or broom handle, and I always have a walking stick, usually a bo, a jo staff, or a hiking staff with me when I am out hiking in the mountains. It just seemed to me to be more practical.

The first part of principle 16 really doesn't apply to modern day warriors, martial artists, and collectors. Almost all of us have a home and have enough room to collect and/or display our weapons. And many of us use them for decorations, as well as enjoy them in our training. So, I will mostly focus on the second part of this principle–do not practice with weapons beyond what is useful.

To be fair, a weapon's usefulness is subjective. If you enjoy taking part in martial arts tournaments, you may find that some of the traditional martial arts weapons are indeed useful for you to practice with. They are useful in your art or your hobby.

I do want to point out that there is a big difference between practicing martial arts as an art or hobby and practicing martial arts for self-defense. It is up to each individual to decide why he or she is actually interested in the martial arts and what he or she wants to get from the training.

If you are training strictly for the art aspect of the martial arts, then you are doing so for fun, an interesting hobby, or your lifestyle. If, on the other hand, you are practicing for real self-defense, then you would want to mostly train with a weapon, or weapons, that actually makes sense for the world in which you live. That is why I chose to train with sticks, knives, and firearms, along with my traditional martial arts training.

In the past, if you said that you were a martial artist or a black belt, that meant that you absolutely could defend yourself, with or without a weapon. Today, martial arts are not the same as they used to be; they have been watered down. Many martial arts instructors cannot defend themselves on the streets and have never been in an actual fight. But that is a totally separate topic.

As we know, Musashi's martial arts practice was serious. His training meant the difference between life and death. So, he took his training deadly serious. If a technique or a weapon was not useful in defeating his opponent, he considered it a waste of time.

The rest of this chapter will be focused mostly on self-defense aspects of the martial arts, as that is where Musashi's focus was when he wrote this principle. And, unlike some of the other principles, this principle is straightforward and to the point.

Not practicing with weapons beyond what is useful can mean more than simply not practicing with a weapon that you would not use for self-defense. A martial artist's hands and feet are also weapons; this principle can also apply to your practice session itself. If you push yourself past a certain point in your practice session, to where you are exhausted, especially with a weapon, you stand a chance of getting sloppy with your techniques.

That is also when you stand a greater chance of losing your focus or possibly injuring yourself. It is not only your body that tires during a long, strenuous practice session, but also your mind. Losing focus during a long, hard practice session, especially with a bladed weapon, is not the smartest thing you can do.

There is a time to train to total exhaustion, but those training sessions are for a specific reason. This type of training is what the samurai called shugyo, which means austere training. This is a strenuous, concentrated, and intensive period of training. It is not something that you do very often. It serves as extensive training to push yourself to the very limit and you must be prepared for it or you could injure yourself.

Training with your weapon for self-defense is not really a part of shugyo training; this would not be considered useful. Also, if you train past a certain point, you start to get diminishing returns on your training session. Every martial artist has had a hard training session that leaves him tired and exhausted. This is not what I am referring to as shugyo training; shugyo training lasts for hours.

Keep your mind on your reason for training. If you are training for self-defense, then over-training is not only unproductive for you, but could cause an injury. And injuring yourself by over-training is detrimental to your goal of being prepared for a life-or-death attack on the streets. After all, a man with an injury is a much easier target than one who is rested and 100 percent ready for an attack.

Musashi obviously knew this. For him, over-training and sustaining an injury could have possibly meant death. Remember, Musashi lived in the 1600s. During this period in Japan, fighting duels with other samurai was not the only danger. People had to contend with bandits and more. Any injury placed him at a disadvantage.

This principle also demonstrates Musashi's philosophy that it is better to master one or two weapons than to try to master many different weapons. Of course, as a former samurai, Musashi would have had a working knowledge of many different weapons, but like most samurai, it was important to be a master of the sword.

And, as we discovered in the last principle, Musashi did not believe in accumulating material possessions without a specific purpose. He focused only on what was practical and useful.

Musashi gave us insight into his philosophy on martial arts in *The Book of Five Rings*, saying, "The true science of martial arts means practicing them in such a way that they will be useful at any time, and to teach them in such a way that they will be useful in all things." He did not believe in wasted effort or wasted time. If he thought that a certain weapon was not as useful to him, then he did not want to waste his time training with it.

He is teaching us, once again, to avoid excess possessions by focusing on what is truly necessary. Musashi knew it is more important to master a few weapons than to simply be familiar with many. Decide which weapons make sense for your purpose and then master those weapons. It is better to be an expert with one or two weapons than to be familiar with many, but a master of none.

It is completely up to each practitioner which weapons he chooses to train with during his training. But, if you are training for true self-defense, I would advise you to only train with the weapons that are useful for self-defense in today's world, and I think Musashi would agree with this.

What weapons would this be? Well, when you get right down to it, anything can be used as a weapon, but not too many people train to defend themselves with a remote control or rolled up newspaper. I would recommend learning the art of the stick, how to use a firearm for self-defense, and some knife training. And yes, you do need to know more than "the end with the hole in it is the dangerous end" or "the pointy end goes in the other guy." Your training must be deadly serious, because one day it may just save your life.

Study strategy over the years and achieve the spirit of the warrior.
Miyamoto Musashi

Principle 17
Do not fear death.

The admonition to not fear death is wisdom that has been taught throughout the ages. Death is simply a part of living; everything and everybody who lives on this planet must experience death at one point in time. It is inevitable, and as such, why should we fear it?

Musashi knew this. In fact, being a samurai, and then a ronin, meant that Musashi's lifespan was much more unpredictable than most people. A samurai could be ordered to commit seppuku by his daimyo at any time, and he would have to comply. Musashi's life was in the hands of his lord until he became a ronin.

Even after he became a ronin, he risked his life repeatedly, at least 60 times that we know of, in fights to the death. If he had lost his focus or accidentally slipped during one of his fights, his life would have been over immediately. Living life as he did meant he had to be prepared for death at any time.

Musashi understood that life was temporary and unpredictable. He also knew that the fear of death would affect his mind, and that would affect the way he fought. He had to be calm, focused, and fearless to fight at a superior level.

He embraced death, as did most samurai. Musashi realized the impermanence of life and lived his life fully and fearlessly, by his own rules. Think about it. Musashi blatantly scoffed at many of the samurai traditions and was overly cocky about it.

The way he approached many of his duels was akin to spitting in the face of not only the samurai traditions, but the actual swordsman that he was facing. And he did so purposely to anger his opponent and to gain an advantage. This must have put him at odds with the samurai everywhere he traveled; they probably wanted him humiliated, defeated, and headless.

He knew that the fear of death could prey on the warrior's mind and weaken his resolve, and as such, it would make death and defeat an even greater possibility. When one fears death, it affects his courage and bravery; he cannot live life to the fullest or fight as freely as he should and be afraid of dying.

We are told that Musashi killed his first man when he was only 13 years old. That is very young to come to terms with death. What we must realize is that Musashi did not grow up like most kids do today. He was raised his whole life to be a samurai, so he was taught at an early age not to fear death and that he should seek an honorable death as the samurai before him did.

Musashi knew that, although he did not seek death, he must be ready to die at any time. He knew he had to be prepared for death at all times. Musashi stated it clearly, saying, "To win any battle, you must fight as if you are already dead." This is just a part of being a warrior, not only in the 16th and 17th centuries, but today as well. Nobody is guaranteed to live a long life.

Although we do not have to be concerned about some self-important daimyo commanding us to commit suicide, this principle applies to us as much as it did to Musashi. If you allow your fears to control your life, you cannot live life to the fullest. You must confront and conquer all your fears to free yourself from them and live the life that you are meant to live. You simply cannot allow your fears to guide your path.

The paradox of death is, while no one in their right mind wants to die before he has lived a full life, fearing death prevents you from living life to the fullest. After all, you can't live life to the fullest and fear death at the same time. You must confront your mortality and live free of the fear of death. But how do you do that?

The samurai accepted death as a part of their life. They meditated on their death and kept their death in the forefront of their mind each day. That may seem a bit morbid, but if you think about it, it makes perfect sense. Isn't that the basis of every religion when you get right down to it?

The various religions are concerned with living life in such a way as to ensure that you do not have to worry about what happens to you after the death of your physical body. In Christianity, you are taught that accepting Jesus as your savior will ensure that you go to Heaven. In Buddhism, you are taught that living a certain way ensures a better reincarnation.

Each religion has its own requirements and teachings concerning what you must do to guarantee a pleasant afterlife; that is the principal focus of almost all religions. Therefore, the central purpose of a religion is to teach you how to live your life in such a way that you will live a good life on earth and enjoy a peaceful, pleasant life after the death of your physical body.

People have been meditating on their own death for thousands of years. It is not morbid to think about your death; it is simply a part of being human. And it is a necessary part in order to get past your fear of death. Think about it. How do most religions convert new members to their faith? By using the fear of death.

Christians convert others to their religion by telling them if they do not believe in Jesus, and accept him as their lord and savior, they will go to Hell and live a tortured life for all eternity. People become Buddhist because they are concerned about being reincarnated as a dung beetle or some lower life form, so they want to learn how to live their life to be assured of a good reincarnation.

If you examine most religions, you will discover that they were established to answer questions concerning what happens when we die and how we should live to have a peaceful, happy life, both on earth and after death. But after most people convert to their chosen religion, they stop giving their death much thought and simply focus on living their life by the teachings of their religion. And many don't even give their daily actions much thought.

Although most people know they are not guaranteed a long life, they put that thought out of their mind. The samurai did not have that luxury. You might say that the samurai took their thoughts about death more seriously because they lived with the constant awareness that each day might be their last.

And even though you are not a samurai, and you don't have a feudal lord that holds your life in his hands, I have news for you–you also live with the constant possibility of death. The only difference is that people today prefer to put those thoughts out of their mind and not to think about the possibility that each day could be their last.

That said, you should be as prepared to meet death as Musashi was. A long life is not guaranteed to anyone on this earth. None of us know how much time we have left to live. Very few people expect to die anytime soon, but every single day, people of all ages die unexpectedly. This is just a fact of life. The question then, is how do we live our lives to the fullest, knowing that death could come for us at any moment?

One thing that the samurai did, which is a good practice for everyone, is that they always kept their affairs in order. Since they never knew when they would die, they did not let things slide. They were very organized and kept their paperwork, etc. ready in case of their death. This is something that you should consider as well.

Most of us are so busy with jobs, family, responsibilities, hobbies, training, etc., that we never think about keeping things organized and prepared for our death. But having your affairs in order is one of the simplest things that you can do to put your mind at ease. It brings one a lot of peace knowing that his family will be taken care of in the event of his death.

Also, don't be afraid to meditate on your death. Take the time to realistically come to terms with the fact that you will die. Get your spiritual life in order. You should know what you believe and why. What are your spiritual beliefs? How strongly to believe what you have been taught? Are you secure with your beliefs about what happens after you die?

These are all important questions to consider. By coming to terms with your spiritual life, you will remove much of your fear of death. However, to be at peace with your death, you must take the time to meditate on these things and truly understand what you believe and why.

Meditating on your death will put your life in perspective. If you do this, you will find that it will put your mind at ease, and you will have a calm spirit about your inevitable death. It will enable you to live your life more fully, and with more purpose and meaning. Also, it will allow you to spend whatever time you have left with no regrets, because you will continually be reminded of the urgency of living every day, every hour, and every minute to the fullest.

Every culture throughout history has had to come to grips with the impermanence of life on this earth. If you study spiritual wisdom as I do, you will find that there is an abundance of teachings about death and how to accept it with a peaceful spirit. Find the philosophy or teachings that align with your spirit and come to a peaceful resolution concerning your own death.

You are on this planet for a specific reason. While you may or may not know what your purpose is, I can guarantee you it is not to tiptoe around fearing your death.

Death is merely a transition, not the end of your life. There are many books available which get in-depth about life after death. Some of the oldest books that we know of are centered on what happens after you die. Also, you may find it helpful to do some research on those who have had what are called near-death experiences. These are very interesting.

I have read many of the books concerning near-death experiences, and there are many things which people who have died and been revived have in common. I will not go into a whole lot of detail concerning these accounts, but I will say that the most common thing people who have come back say is that their experience was very peaceful, tranquil, and loving.

They felt surrounded by a feeling which they could only describe as love. These people described being in a place of love, and many say that they were with God or Jesus. Some say that they were given the choice about whether to come back to earth or to stay where they were. Many describe seeing a bright, white light and a tunnel, and others described hearing music and seeing colors that were so beautiful they did not have the words to describe them.

One thing that almost all of them stated was that they no longer had any fear of death. Many stated that they actually look forward to dying and returning to where they had been. In addition, all of them came back with a different outlook on life. They related a more loving and giving attitude, and a tremendous feeling of inner peace; the experience completely changed their lives.

What makes these people's experiences even more believable is the fact that many of these people work in the medical profession. They understand the different theories about what happens to the body and the brain when someone dies. Some of these books are actually written by a doctor who had a near death experience.

If you find that the fear of death is something that is plaguing your mind, you may find it helpful to read some of these books and compare what these people say with whatever religious or spiritual beliefs that you have about life and death. I guarantee you will find them interesting.

No matter what you believe about death, you must come to terms with the fact that it is not only military personnel, or those with very dangerous jobs, whose lives are on the line every single day. You are not guaranteed tomorrow; nobody is. Death awaits each of us. Today is the day to prepare for your death, especially if you find that you have a fear of death.

The Japanese Buddhist priest, Shinsho, around 400 years before Musashi's time, put it this way: "No matter what road I travel,

I'm going home." There are many theories on death, but Dag Hammarskjold wrote some great advice for warriors. He stated, "Do not seek death. Death will find you. But seek the road which makes death a fulfillment."

What is the road that will make death a fulfillment? It is the road of a life lived to the fullest, making the most of every day. That road is filled with good actions, helping others as much as you can, and living the best life you can, with honor, integrity, character, and, above all, love for your fellow man.

The *Bible* states, "Let us love one another, for love is from God, and whoever loves has been born of God and knows God. Anyone who does not love does not know God, because God is love." This fits perfectly with what many, who have had near-death experiences, say about what they felt when they died.

Sages and philosophers throughout the ages have discussed death and how one should look at dying. Socrates puts your mind at ease, saying: "Death may be the greatest of all human blessings." And Marcus Aurelius wrote, "Death smiles at us all, all a man can do is smile back."

Why fear what is not only inevitable, but that every living being on this planet experiences? The day that you are born is the day that you start to die. Life is not independent from death; it only appears that way. Every single hour you live is one hour closer to the minute of your death.

Living in fear of this does not change it; it only robs you of the joy and freedom of living your life in the present moment. The fear of death does not prevent you from dying; it prevents you from living your life to the fullest. Live your life in such a way that you no longer fear death; live with honor, integrity, and love!

The Way of the warrior is resolute acceptance of death.
Miyamoto Musashi

Principle 18
Do not seek to possess either goods or fiefs for your old age.

Principle 18 is another one of those principles that you must read with regard to both the time period and the lifestyle in which Musashi lived. Let's deal with the time period issue first.

As you already know, Musashi lived in the 16th and 17th centuries. The historical research has found that during this period in Japan, the life expectancy was only 35 years old. And it was even less for a samurai. The average life expectancy of a samurai was only 25 years! This makes Musashi's life even more interesting since he was 63 years old when he died.

Additionally, Musashi was a wanderer and never married or had a family of his own. Even if he had accumulated any valuable possessions or land, he had no loved ones to leave any belongings to. His last text, the *Dokkodo*, translates as the way of walking alone, the way of the lone warrior, or the way of self-reliance, depending on the translation.

When you put the *Dokkodo* in the context of the period in which Musashi lived, and his status as a ronin, it is easy to see why this principle would apply to Musashi's life and maybe the lives of his students. After all, why would someone who did not figure to live very long, and who had no wife or children, seek to acquire many possessions, wealth, or land for his old age?

Musashi knew full well that he could not take any possessions or land with him when he died, and he had no one to leave an estate of land or wealth to at his death. In addition, he knew that his only legacy would be his name and his writings, both of which have lived on for centuries after his death.

Out of his 21 principles, this one probably applies to our modern-day culture the least, as our life expectancy is more than double what the average life expectancy was during Musashi's lifetime. It is wise for us to have some belongings and a home, and to save some wealth for our old age. In fact, it is absolutely necessary to prevent us from living in poverty later in life.

Today, the longer we live, the more we need a safe place to live and money for food, clothes, medical bills, etc. It would be foolish for us not to prepare for our old age. Also, most people want to leave something for their children and grandchildren. As the *Book of Proverbs* states, "A good man leaves an inheritance to his grandchildren."

Musashi did not have any of these considerations; he lived for the day, not concerning himself about tomorrow. As I already discussed, he spent the last two years of his life living in a cave. I don't know about anyone else, but personally, I don't want to live the last two years of my life, or any years of my life, living in a cave. That is just not the world that we live in today.

One of the issues that we see quite often today is misguided people who seek to judge men of the past by today's standards. This is complete idiocy! You can only seek to understand someone from a different period by the wisdom, culture, and standards of his day. Think about it. How would you like it if your actions today were judged by someone's standards 200, 300, or 400 years from now? Only simpletons would even consider such a thing!

If we were to do that with Musashi, then, instead of a wise martial arts icon, we would see him as a selfish rogue and a murderer. We would see the samurai culture as elitists who abused the lower class and murdered anyone who showed them the slightest disrespect. But neither the samurai nor Musashi lived in our time, and their culture and standards differed vastly from our own.

In order to truly understand Musashi, and the samurai, we must study them from their own culture and standards, not from our culture and standards. We must look beyond what Musashi wrote and seek to understand the reasoning behind his teachings.

Even today, diverse cultures in different parts of the world are vastly different. Their customs and beliefs are different; their morals, standards, and laws are different. Their religions are different, and their lives are different. It is wrong to judge a wolf by the same standards that you would judge a lap dog.

That said, Principle 18 is not as useful for us today as most of Musashi's other principles. We do need to plan for our future and our old age. You don't want to be an 80-year-old man with no food, no medical care, and no place to live.

On the other hand, if we read between the lines, we can find some wisdom even in this principle. While we do need to prepare for our future, we shouldn't spend all our time planning for retirement or our old age. Doing so would mean that you are wasting a large portion of your life.

We must plan for the future, while living each day to the fullest. If we postpone traveling or enjoying life until we are older, there will probably be many things that we are unable to do. Many people make this mistake. They scrimp and save every penny for when they are older, but then their health is not good, or they suffer from injuries which prohibit them from doing the things that they always dreamed of doing.

You must be wise and plan for your future, while learning from the past, and living life to the fullest in the present moment. If you spend too much time on any of these aspects of your life, you will find that your life is unbalanced. If you only focus on saving for the future, you won't live fully in the present. If you spend too much time and money having fun in the present, you are sacrificing the quality of your life in the future. Balance is the key.

Life is about learning from your past experiences, using that wisdom and knowledge to improve your present, and planning for your future. Many people believe that life is short, so they should live it up right now and not worry about the future. But this is shortsighted. This line of thought is why so many elderly people are living the latter years of their lives in poverty, their days spent sitting alone in front of a television. That is a sad life, and you don't want to live like this.

Gain wisdom and knowledge while you are young. Work hard and play hard. Start a family and enjoy your life. Start saving and invest a portion of your income every week. You won't really miss the money that you set aside during those years, but when you are older, I promise you will be extremely happy that you were wise enough to plan for your future, instead of only living for the day. You must think long term.

I hear so many people saying things such as, "You can't take it with you," or "I don't plan on living very long anyway." This kind of attitude may be enjoyable now, but it is extremely unwise. While it is true that you can't take your money with you, it is also true that you can't buy food or pay bills with wishes and fairy dust. Live and enjoy your life in the present, but plan for the future!

You don't have any idea how long your life will be. With the breakthroughs in medical technology today, your life expectancy may be much longer than you expect. Don't gamble with your latter years; they will be here sooner than you think.

As you live your life, you will find that all the fun you have had in the past is meaningless in the present moment. It might make for a few good memories, but that is all. If you are younger, you may think it is smart to live it up now, but I can promise you, nothing comes for free. Everything has a cost.

If you are living it up now, you will pay for it later. Spending all your money and not planning for the future will catch up with you eventually. Partying hard in your twenties may seem fun, but when the bill comes due in your 50s or 60s, you will wish that you were wiser during your early years.

Nobody rides for free! If you don't take care of your body when you are young, you will be forced to pay the tab when you are older. And when you are older, you won't care how much fun you had in your twenties; those memories won't pay the bills or heal the damage that you have done to your body.

There is an old Japanese proverb which states, "For good judgment, ask old people." If you ask any elderly person, they will tell you to plan well for your future and start investing as early as possible. Think about it. If you had bought 1,000 shares of Amazon when it went public in 1997, that investment would be worth $1.1 million today, and that does not include all the stock splits!

You are not Musashi, you do not live in feudal Japan, and you don't want to spend your older years in a cave. Be wise, not foolhardy. Plan for the future, while learning from the past, and living life to the fullest in the present moment!

A man cannot understand the art he is studying
if he only looks for the end result without taking the
time to delve deeply into the reasoning of the study.
Miyamoto Musashi

Principle 19
Respect Buddha and the gods without counting on their help.

When you think of Musashi, religion or God is not the first thing that comes to mind. After all, it is hard to consider a man who traveled from place-to-place fighting duels to the death as being very spiritual. And to be fair, we really do not know that much about Musashi's spiritual beliefs or practices.

That said, as you read through Musashi's 21 Principles, it becomes clear that Musashi most likely had spiritual beliefs and practices. He spent the last two years of his life living in a cave, meditating and writing. You don't spend that much time meditating and in personal reflection and not have some spiritual beliefs or practices.

The predominant religion in Japan was Shintoism, dating back to somewhere between 1,000 b.c. to 300 b.c. It is basically a religion centered on ancestor worship. Shinto means the way of the gods, and the gods in Shintoism are called kami. It was thought that after humans died, they became kami and then were revered by their families as ancestral kami or spiritual deities. Shintoism is still practiced by many in Japan today.

The other dominant religion during Musashi's day was Mahayana Buddhism. It was introduced to Japan around the year 550 from Korea. It wasn't until the 13th century that the Japanese monk, Dogen, brought Soto Zen to Japan. Dogen is considered one of the great Buddhist philosophers and his teaching quickly spread throughout Japan, influencing the whole Japanese culture.

All of this happened before Musashi's time, so we can presume that he was most likely influenced by each of these religious beliefs to some degree, and that they formed the basis of whatever spiritual beliefs he may have had. Musashi obviously had respect for both Buddhism and Shintoism, according to Principle 19.

Since Musashi most likely grew up in a family who practiced at least one of these religions, we can also assume that he had witnessed many occasions where those he knew had prayed for help with certain things and their prayers went unanswered. Because of this, he was wise enough to understand that you can't simply count on your religious beliefs alone; you must act and take responsibility for your own life. You must work hard to get what you want.

Today, we have many more religions than Musashi could have imagined. Nonetheless, his sage advice in Principle 19 still holds true for us in our modern lives. Pay respect to whatever religion or spiritual beliefs that you adhere to, but don't count on God to always do everything for you. You must be willing to put forth the effort to accomplish what you want in life.

In the first part of this principle, Musashi tells us to respect Buddha and the gods. How do you go about respecting God? The first step is adhering to your religious beliefs. If you are a Buddhist, you respect Buddhism by living according to the teachings of Buddha. If you are a Christian, you respect Jesus and God by adhering to the teachings of Jesus in the Bible. If you are Jewish, you respect God by living according to the teachings of the Hebrew Bible.

Whatever religion you observe, you respect it by following the decrees and teachings of that religion, whether that is showing respect to your ancestors, meditating on the religious teachings, or praying.

While your spiritual life is important, it does not take the place of working for what you want in life. Musashi knew this, as the second part of this principle states, "without counting on their help." There is a popular maxim that states, "God helps those who help themselves," and this is basically what Musashi is saying in Principle 19.

You should have respect for, and faith in, your spiritual beliefs, but that does not relieve you of your duty and responsibility to work for what you want. Don't simply count on God to help make everything right if you are not willing to put in the work.

Musashi believed you should respect your spiritual beliefs, but that you shouldn't allow your spiritual practices or beliefs to be the cause of your laziness or inaction. He understood he had to train hard to hone his martial arts skills to survive the duels that he fought. Musashi didn't simply pray to magically be anointed with those skills; he had to work hard for them over years and years of training.

Look at it this way. If you are going to war, you may absolutely want to pray for God's blessing and protection on the battlefield.

But if you simply prayed for God's protection and disregarded your training and common sense during the battle, you should not expect that God is going to magically save you. Pray, have faith, and give respect to God, but use your brain, your training, and some common sense!

Think about the story of David and Goliath. David was a man who obviously respected God and asked for God's protection throughout his life. When David was on the battlefield, as a teenager, facing an experience warrior of impressive statue, of course he prayed for God's protection. But he had to step up, choose the right stones for his slingshot, and use the skill set that he had honed over many years as a shepherd to kill Goliath.

David didn't simply step on the battlefield with no experience under his belt and expect to bring down his enemy's greatest warrior. He had already put in the work and knew he had the necessary skills to kill Goliath; *then* he asked God for his blessings and protection, and to *help* him defeat Goliath.

He didn't simply step out to meet his enemy and hope that God would somehow magically cause Goliath to trip and fall on his sword or something. He knew he had done the work to hone his skills, and he had faith that he could kill this giant warrior. It was only after he had prepared that he asked for God's protection.

We can assume that Musashi asked for blessings from the kami or from Buddha before his duels, but we don't know. What we do know is that Musashi used every means at his disposal to defeat each of his opponents; he didn't merely count on the kami or Buddha to win his duels for him.

We can also assume, without much doubt, that if Musashi had simply prayed to the kami or Buddha to keep him safe and had gone into those duels with no preparation or training, that he would not have survived very long. There are no shortcuts. He had to apply himself and do the work!

For another example, consider someone testing for his black belt. That person would have to put in years of training with his instructor, and a lot of practice outside of the dojo, to pass his test. If, instead of putting in years of blood, sweat, and tears in hard practice sessions, he simply prayed for God to help him pass the test and not get injured, do you think he could pass the black belt test? Of course not! He did not do his part.

It is good to have a spiritual practice and pray for God's help and protection; but you also must step up and do your part. I can't think of any religion that I have studied where you are taught to simply do nothing and count on God to take care of everything for you. God put you on this earth for a reason, and you may not know what that reason is, but I am completely sure that it was not to sit on your butt and expect God to provide everything for you while you do nothing.

Meditate, trust in God, respect your chosen spiritual practices, but work to achieve your goals in life. There is an old Arab proverb which states, "Trust God, but tie your camel." And this is what Musashi is trying to get across to us.

Consider the story of the man who was caught in a massive flood. It had rained for days and days, and the entire area was flooded. The water rose over the top of many homes. One man was stranded on top of the roof of his house. So he prayed to God to save him.

Soon, a boat came by and stopped and asked if he wanted a ride. The man replied, "No, I am fine. God will save me." About an hour later, a guy came by on a jet ski and stopped to save the man. Again, the man said, "No thank you. God will save me.

It was almost dark when the man heard a helicopter flying overhead with a spotlight shining on him. The pilot lowered a ladder so the man could climb to safety, but the man refused, saying, "No. I am fine. God will provide for me."

The man drowned two hours later and found himself in Heaven speaking with God. The man said, "God, why didn't you save me? I prayed and prayed, but you didn't come for me."

Then God said, "Well, I sent you a boat, a jet ski, and a helicopter. Why didn't you take action and save yourself? You did not do your part."

Trust in God, but be willing to do the work. Don't count on a supernatural miracle to change your life; that is up to you. If you want something, you must take the personal responsibility and work for it. It doesn't matter if it is martial arts skills or a new profession, respect God, pray, and live as you should, but you still must do the work.

Perceive that which cannot be seen with the eye.
Miyamoto Musashi

Principle 20
You may abandon your own body but you must preserve your honor.

This is one of the most important principles of the *Dokkodo*. Musashi was raised in a samurai family, and as such, he understood the importance of maintaining your honor no matter what. When you value your honor, that does not change because you have a major change in your life, like Musashi becoming a ronin.

Self-respect and honor were of the utmost importance to a samurai; he would rather die than live with dishonor. Musashi is urging us to maintain our honor, even to the point of death. This is something that most people in today's world have a hard time understanding. Honor is not something that most people even give much thought to today. But true warriors look at honor a bit differently.

Even though few people value their honor above their life in today's culture, this principle still holds a lot of wisdom for everyone. To respect yourself, you must stay true to your values and beliefs. When someone compromises their core principles, it damages his self-respect, self-esteem, and ultimately, his self-confidence. You must live authentically, according to your own personal code, to have true self-respect.

Always do what you feel is right, even if everyone else disagrees with you. It is essential that you follow your own code and moral beliefs about what is right and what is wrong. What someone else thinks about your beliefs, or your actions, is of no consequence. Others' beliefs and opinions apply to them; your beliefs and code of honor are all that should matter to you.

It is when friends and family strongly disagree with your beliefs that your devotion to your own principles is tested. Most of us are not concerned with whether or not some stranger agrees with our actions; it is when those closest to you pressure you about your choices that you have to stand strong on your own principles and ethics. You must be completely devoted to your personal code of honor to stand strong when the pressure is on you.

That said, most people have never even stopped to think about what they truly stand for, what honor means to them, or whether they should even have a code of honor. Most of our population only considers honor when it comes to the honor code of their school, but there is much more to your personal honor than that. Your school's honor code is your school's code of ethics; it really has nothing to do with your own personal ethics.

Everyone should take the time to think about his own code of honor–what he feels is right or wrong. Does this mean that everyone can just randomly decide what is right or wrong in their life, while disregarding long-held values and principles of the world? Of course not! Some thug may decide that, according to his code, stealing is perfectly acceptable. That would not mean that stealing is an honorable act, not for him or anyone else.

There are certain values that are universal, and you cannot simply decide that they don't apply to you. It is not honorable to steal, murder, rape, or abuse other people. Some principles that are set in stone. There is a difference between developing your own honor code or principles, and in deciding that nothing is wrong for you if you say it isn't wrong.

There are universal principles that must apply to every honorable man, whether he likes them or not. Murder and rape are dishonorable no matter how much some criminal may try to justify his actions. Lying for personal gain and cheating other people is a dishonorable act, period. But what about lying to save someone's life or stealing from an enemy's camp during a war?

There are some principles which are set in stone and other principles which are subjective. This is why it is very important for you to take the time to reflect on your own code of honor. What are your core values? If an action is wrong in some circumstances, but acceptable in other situations, you must be crystal clear concerning those issues.

For example, during wartime, it is absolutely acceptable to lie and mislead your enemy or to steal his supplies. Sun Tzu taught in the *Art of War* that, "All warfare is based on deception." But how do you balance that if your code of honor states that you will not lie?

This is just one example of why it is important to be clear about your personal code of honor. No matter what is or is not in your code of honor, you will find circumstances that will test your clarity and your devotion to your honor code. If you are not clear concerning what you believe, what is right for you, and what actions are unacceptable for you, you will falter when pressured or faced with a serious situation which challenges your beliefs in some way.

It is vital that you stay true to your personal beliefs and live authentically, but that is hard to do if you don't take the time to know what you believe and why. Living with integrity means living according to your own principles. If you have never stopped to think about what your principles are, how can you live with integrity?

Musashi obviously lived by his own code of honor, even when other samurai condemned many of his dueling tactics. The condemnation of others did not faze him in the least because he had decided what honor meant to him and he followed his code. He did what he thought was right, regardless of the consequences or what others thought about his actions.

This is how everyone should live their life. Decide what is acceptable to you and what isn't, and then have the integrity to live according to your own principles and uphold your honor. Refuse to compromise your principles or your honor. This is easy to agree to but can be very hard to live up to at times.

One way to uphold your honor is to make a firm decision to never do anything that you can't live with or that does not feel right to your conscience. While your beliefs are important, it is your actions that make you who you truly are. Beliefs mean nothing if they don't lead to right actions. You must live in such a way that you respect yourself as a man or woman of honor.

If you have a firm belief about what constitutes your honor, and you act contrary to that belief, you will start to lose respect for yourself, and that will have a snowball effect in your life. The less you respect yourself, the more likely you are to compromise your principles and the less your honor will mean to you. And the less your honor means to you, the more you will continue to compromise on your beliefs and principles.

If you get caught up in this cycle, it won't be long before you find you are no longer an honorable person; you simply change your beliefs and principles according to the situation. That is situational ethics and is the opposite of upholding your honor. Honor doesn't change simply because you find yourself in a tight spot or because everyone is urging you to compromise your principles. This is what Musashi is trying to get across to us, by saying that you must preserve honor even if it means giving up your life. That doesn't leave much doubt about how important your principles and honor should be to you!

Your honor and integrity must be a priority for you. It is essential to uphold your moral and ethical principles to maintain your honor and self-respect. Once you lose your self-respect, your honor will mean very little to you; you will compromise your principles anytime it is to your advantage.

If your honor and code of ethics are not a priority for you, it will become all too easy to lower your standards when your back is against the wall. You must live with integrity and make all your decisions align with your core principles and your code of honor. If your decisions don't align with your values, then you are not living a life of honor.

Additionally, you must make your decisions rationally; don't allow your emotions or biases to dictate your decisions. You must always be in the be mindful of your honor. If you get caught up in the moment, it's easy to forget about your honor and just go with the flow. Stay mindful and always maintain your honor, even in the smallest decisions. If you do this, maintaining your honor becomes a habit and will be much easier to uphold.

I want to make one last point concerning honor. Being a man or woman of honor does not guarantee that you will maintain a spotless reputation. Your reputation not only depends on your actions and the way you live your life, but on the opinions of other people, many who are not honorable people themselves. Remember, you only have control over your own thoughts and actions, not what other people think or say about you.

Your reputation is what other people think about you; your honor depends exclusively on you, not the opinions of others. While it is nice to have a good reputation, that should not be the deciding factor when it comes to your actions.

Your principles and honor should always guide your actions, not the opinions of other people. Their opinions are none of your business; your responsibility is to uphold your honor, not to worry about what others think about it.

There are those people who will go out of their way to destroy your reputation and try to convince others that you are not a man or woman of honor. These people don't care about the truth; they only care about their own misguided goals or personal vendettas.

When people like that see you doing better than they are, they can become jealous to the point of hating you for being more successful, or even more honorable, than them. Their jealousy can reach the point of a burning hatred of you.

The more honorable you are, the more they will hate you and want to bring you down or somehow prove that you aren't honorable. Your honor reminds them that they do not live as they should; and your success reminds them of their own shortcomings.

In one way, they admire you and would like to live as you do. In another way, they hate the fact that you remind them of how much they have compromised their own honor and principles. It is a strange love/hate relationship that they have with *their image of you.*

I say "their image of you" because they most likely have never met you or communicated with you. How they see you has no basis in reality; it is simply an image which they have created in their own twisted mind. Since they do not live with honor, they erroneously think that your honor must be as fake as their honor is to them.

Musashi dealt with the same type of hatred from many of the samurai of his day. Instead of focusing on upholding their own honor, they complained of Musashi being dishonorable and having disreputable practices. They disagreed with how Musashi conducted himself because *his* conduct did not live up to *their* standards.

You can see this type of jealousy and envy today where certain people spend more time judging others according to their own standards than they do actually living up to those standards themselves.

It is not hard to find examples of this in today's world. There are Muslims who judge non-Muslims according to Muslim standards. Much of the terrorism today revolves around those kinds of misguided convictions. That is no different from judging Musashi's actions according to today's standards.

And this misguided idea of others having to live up to your standards is not limited to Muslims or any one group or religion. It is also easy to find some Christians who judge others according to their own personal Christian beliefs. They seem to conveniently forget what Jesus taught about this topic: "Do not judge others, and you will not be judged. For you will be treated as you treat others. The standard you use in judging is the standard by which you will be judged."

How others live their life, and what standards others live by, is none of your business, as long as they are not hurting others. Your business is making sure that *you* live up to *your* code of honor; it is not ensuring that someone else lives according to your code of honor. If everyone realized this, and lived according to philosophy, we would have a much more peaceful world.

It is not your job to judge others or to ensure that others live how you think they should live. Your only concern should be to make sure that you are living according to your own code of honor. Honor is a personal responsibility. To quote the Scottish hero, Rob Roy, "Honor is what no man can give you and none can take away. Honor is a man's gift to himself."

Although nobody can take your honor from you, you can give it away by compromising your principles and not living up to your code of honor. Maintaining your honor depends totally on you; it doesn't matter what anyone else thinks about it or says about it. Their opinions concerning your honor are meaningless, and you should not be overly concerned about what they think.

When you preserve your honor at all costs, then you are a man of honor, no matter what anyone else says or thinks about it. Discipline yourself to be a man of honor. Refuse to lower your standards for anyone or any reason.

Furthermore, don't fall into the trap of judging others by your standards. You were not put on this earth to judge others, but to live your own life by your own standards. Your honor is a personal issue and should not be held as a standard for anyone besides yourself. Live your life your way and allow others to do the same.

In the end, it is your stubborn refusal to compromise your principles that makes you a man of honor. No one else can give you this, and no one else can take it away from you. It is you, and you alone, who must discipline yourself to take a stand and live your life according to your own code of honor, just as Musashi did. Never compromise where your honor is concerned.

If there isn't discipline, how can
there be a true realization of an ideal?
Miyamoto Musashi

Principle 21
Never stray from the way.

I have seen many people on the internet interpret this principle as your own chosen path in life, but that is not what Musashi was referring to when he wrote never stray from the way. As with many old texts, some people try to get a little too philosophical about the *Dokkodo* in order to make it fit into other ideas or subjects to make money.

Since Musashi did not expand on his 21 principles, I guess people could accuse me of being too philosophical concerning the *Dokkodo* as well. My purpose is not to put a new twist on these principles, but to give the reader some insight into Musashi's life and to show how these principles apply to our life today. As with all my writings, I just write what I believe and interpret everything from my own point of view.

That said, Musashi was not referring to "the way" as another way of saying your chosen path, but rather the way of the warrior. The *Dokkodo* translates into "The Way of Walking Alone" or "The Way of the Lone Warrior," which is how Musashi lived his life. Musashi chose to be a ronin and a nomad. His way *was* the way of a lone warrior. So there is very little doubt concerning what he meant by "the way."

When he stated one should never stray from the way, Musashi meant never stray from the path of the warrior and the principles that he set forth in the *Dokkodo*, which were his reflections on how he lived his life, and his last instructions for his students.

Musashi's way of the warrior differed from many of the samurai's ways, while at the same time, integrating many of the samurai's teachings into his philosophy. Principle 21 could be compared to a summary at the end of a text. He just laid out the way of walking alone in 20 precepts, and in the last principle, he is telling us to never stray from these principles.

People like to take old texts from warriors such as Sun Tzu and Musashi and then put their own spin on them to make them apply to other subjects for which they were not meant. For example, many people have taken Sun Tzu's *Art of War* and applied the principles in it to business and other aspects of life. But that does not change the fact that *The Art of War* was written as a strategic manual for warfare.

Musashi did not write the *Dokkodo* to apply to all walks of life, but to summarize how he lived his life as a lone warrior. It was written for his students and those who wanted to learn his way–the way of the lone warrior. That is why we have a hard time making some principles of the *Dokkodo* apply to us in our modern culture.

We live in a completely different world than Musashi. Our world has evolved in such a way that he could have never imagined. Even my grandfather could never have imagined the world as it is today; that is how fast our world is changing.

Yet, we can still apply most of the principles in the *Dokkodo* to our modern lives. And to be completely accurate about what Musashi meant by never straying from the way, we must discuss it in terms of the way of the warrior or bushido, because that is the context in which Musashi meant it.

The warrior lives by different standards than most people in our world. He has disciplined himself to live the warrior lifestyle, and he applies that discipline to every area of his life. This does not necessarily mean that you will find him fighting in some martial arts tournament. The warrior develops his martial arts skills for a specific purpose–to defend himself and those he loves from whoever or whatever may be a threat to them.

Furthermore, the way of the warrior involves much more than the ability to fight or to defend yourself, and that is what Musashi is teaching us with the principles in the *Dokkodo*. Musashi wrote the *Dokkodo* just one week before his death, and as I stated, we can consider it to be his reflections over his lifetime. Most of these principles have little to do with martial arts; they are concerned with how one should live one's life.

We know Musashi focused on more than his martial art skills over his lifetime. As you already know, he became interested in painting, art, philosophy, poetry, calligraphy, and teaching his students. He painted 25 paintings and is considered a genius for not only his martial strategies, but for his artwork as well. Writing had been a part of his life since his early 20s. Although Musashi was a loner and a ronin, he had a full, balanced life, which he could reflect on during his last days. The *Dokkodo* was born out of those reflections.

With all of that considered, we can safely assume that *The Way of the Lone Warrior*, or the *Dokkodo*, reflects how he had lived his life and the principles that he held as important for a warrior of honor and integrity. We can also safely assume that he wrote the *Dokkodo* for his followers and martial art students who wanted to learn his strategies and philosophy. After all, he had no way of knowing that millions of people would read his work hundreds of years later.

Most people become more subdued, reflective, and amiable as they age, and we can see this in the 21 principles of the *Dokkodo*. For example, after killing so many people in sword duels, we can assume that Musashi must have had some regrets over the years, but he cautions us to not regret what we have done.

Anyone who has taken some time and seriously reflected on his life, and some of the things which he has done or neglected to do, has felt the sting of regret. This is just human nature.

At the same time, as he meditates on his regrets, he will eventually come to the realization that regret changes nothing; meditating on regrets only makes him feel sad or depressed. Therefore, the thinking man knows that he should not focus on his regrets. He must accept what he has done and move on with his life.

I believe Musashi went through this same process, urging us to "accept everything just the way it is" and "do not regret what you have done." Both of these principles are wisdom that sages and philosophers have taught throughout the ages. And these principles are just as true today as when Musashi wrote the *Dokkodo*.

After living 63 years, we can be assured that these 21 principles came from Musashi's personal self-reflection during the two years spent in Reigando Cave, meditating, working on his art and his writings. Most elders have a lot of wisdom to share after years of making various mistakes and experiencing different successes. We have no reason to think that Musashi was any different as far as this is concerned.

Musashi's philosophy in the *Dokkodo* is not overly intellectual, and he does not go into detail to explain his principles. This leads us to infer that he thought that these 21 principles were fairly straightforward and that his followers would grasp the wisdom and meaning in each of them, just as he felt his followers would easily understand what he meant by "never stray from the way."

Unlike those of us who read the *Dokkodo* today, Musashi's followers and students actually spent a lot of time listening to Musashi teach about his martial arts strategies and philosophy of life. The teachings in the *Dokkodo* were most likely not something which they had not heard, or been aware of, before Musashi's death. Think about it. If you spend months or years training with your instructor, you will learn much about how he lives and what he truly believes.

There are other Musashi quotes that shed even more light on what he meant by "the way." Consider the following quotes. "One must make the warrior walk his *everyday walk*." "The true science of martial arts means practicing them in such a way that they will be useful at any time, and to teach them in such a way that they will be useful in *all things*." And finally, "If you know *the way* broadly, you will see it *in everything*."

When you reflect on those three quotes, you can easily infer that "the way" that Musashi is referring to is indeed the way of the warrior. If you are making the warrior walk your everyday walk, you are walking, or living, the way of the warrior, or what I call the warrior lifestyle, every day. If you are practicing martial arts so that they will be useful in all things, then the way of the warrior is your lifestyle and you will see aspects of the way in everything, just as Musashi's last quote states.

Musashi is telling us to never stray from the way of the warrior and to be mindful and fully present in each moment. The way of the warrior is not limited to the strategies of dueling or martial arts training; it encompasses every part of your life. It is mindfully living a life of excellence, with honor, integrity, and courage.

The term "the way" is used in many eastern philosophical writings. Lao Tzu's ancient book, *Tao Te Ching*, can roughly be translated as The Way of Virtue. "The way" has different meanings according to the author's philosophical point of view.

To Musashi, "the way" simply refers to the way of the warrior, or bushido, as that is the path that he followed his whole life and the lifestyle which he was teaching to his students. And have no doubts about it, the way of the warrior is a lifestyle. It encompasses every part of your life, not simply your martial arts training. That is why I coined the term "the warrior lifestyle" and use it in most of my books and articles.

When you truly understand the way of the warrior, you know it encompasses an entire lifestyle; it is much more than knowing how to fight and how to defend yourself. Richard Strozzi Heckler, in his book, *In Search of the Warrior Spirit*, stated, "The path of the warrior is lifelong, and mastery is often simply staying on the path." Musashi knew this over 400 years ago and stayed on the warrior path his whole life. And in this principle, he is urging us to never stray from the path of the warrior.

Musashi knew that the warrior's path was not all about war or fighting. He lived a balanced life and integrated the way of the warrior into everything he did.

Most people seem to think that Musashi only lived to fight duels. I have even seen one book written by a misguided group of authors who try to portray Musashi as a psychopath and even a serial killer. They obviously did not do their homework, as he was far from either of those descriptions. After the age of 30, Musashi focused more on mentally dominating his opponents without killing them and stopped taking part in sword fights to the death.

Musashi understood that the warrior should be more than a well-trained fighter. Warriors should lead a balanced life and have more interests in their life than working to perfect their martial arts skills. He knew that followers of "the way" needed balance in their life to be completely fulfilled. Balance is vital for the warrior to be a complete human being. Musashi lived a full life and lived his life by his own code of honor. This is the way of the warrior.

The *Dokkodo* offers a lot of wisdom and a powerful set of principles for us to consider today. These principles urge us to live with a sense of detachment to many aspects of living in the world, but to always maintain our honor. Embracing these principles is a significant starting point for living the warrior lifestyle.

The warrior lifestyle is not only for those in the military or in dangerous jobs, such as law enforcement. Anyone can be a warrior if he or she applies the principles of warriorship to their life and lives a life of honor and integrity. Even Musashi, who no one would argue about whether he was a warrior, stated, "Even if a man has no natural ability, he can be a warrior."

Being a warrior has very little to do with what you do for a profession, and more to do with your attitude and how you live life. I have seen some military guys who lack any semblance of living with honor. Moreover, I have seen ordinary citizens, with no martial arts training whatsoever, courageously risk their life to stand for what is right or to save someone else's life.

Warriorhood isn't what you do for a living; it is about how you live your life and what principles guide your beliefs and your actions. Anyone can live the warrior lifestyle. I have written several books on the warrior lifestyle, and I have readers from every walk of life. Many of my readers are in the military or in law enforcement, but others are teachers, lawyers, martial arts instructors, shamans, preachers, celebrities, essentially, people from all walks of life.

Always remember, being a warrior is not what you do for a living; it is who you are inside. You don't have to look tough or act tough to be a warrior, or to live the warrior lifestyle. It is how you decide to live your life and the principles you adhere to which matter. It is a lifelong path; that is why you should never stray from the way-the way of the warrior.

I am going to end this discussion of Musashi's *Dokkodo* with an excerpt from my book, *Warrior: The Way of Warriorhood.* This book is the best book of the *Warrior Wisdom* series, in my opinion. I don't normally include excerpts from another book when writing a new book, but I think you will find that this excerpt fits perfectly with this discussion.

"The warrior lifestyle involves much more than the ability to fight and defend yourself and those you love. It involves developing your character, living a life of honor and integrity, defending those who can't defend themselves, taking care of the elderly and your family; in short, it involves service to others along with perfecting your character. Many people seem to get hung up on the literal definition of the term "warrior." The literal definition, which can be found in most dictionaries, defines the term "warrior" as someone who is trained or experienced in warfare.

As far as the warrior lifestyle is concerned, this definition falls far short of being complete. Throughout history, when the term "warrior" has been used, it has carried with it a deeper meaning than simply "someone experienced in warfare." Warriors have been revered for their character as much as their martial arts skills. The warrior was seen as a man of character, integrity and honor, not simply someone who knew how to fight, or who was experienced in fighting. It is true that the warrior should be skilled in the art of war or in the martial arts, but this is only a small part of being a true warrior.

Master Gichin Funakoshi, the founder of Shotokan Karate, stated that the ultimate goal of karate is the perfection of one's character, not the perfection of one's martial arts skills. Being a true warrior involves balance. The warrior strives for excellence in every part of his life, not only in developing his martial arts skills, but also in his everyday life. The warrior must endeavor to perfect himself spiritually and mentally, as well as physically. While it is true that the martial arts play an important part in the life of the true warrior, the martial arts are only *a part* of the warrior's life.

There are many other parts of the warrior's life which must also be addressed if he is serious about living the warrior lifestyle. Character training is definitely an important part of being a warrior. Without character training, so-called "warriors" are nothing more than thugs, trained to fight, but with no knowledge of what is worth fighting for. To educate someone in the martial arts without regard to their character, is simply training a menace to society. The ancient martial arts masters knew this and refused to train those who they felt lacked the character and integrity needed to be given these dangerous skills.

Character was important to the masters of old and was considered before someone was trained. Today, the martial arts have become big business and anyone with enough money can obtain as much training as they want, no matter how poor their character may be. Are these people warriors simply because they have purchased years of training and know how to fight? Are gang members, who know how to fight, warriors? Well, if you go by the literal definition, your answer would have to be yes, but if you go by the definition that I use for the true warrior, the answer is definitely no.

My definition of a true warrior is someone who has the ability and will to fight to protect himself, his friends, his family, and his ideals, while at the same time, seeks the perfection of his own character through a life lived with honor, integrity, and an unflinching dedication to what is right according to his own code of honor. The ability to fight is only a small part of this definition. The true warrior must develop more than his martial arts skills; the qualities of the true warrior go much deeper.

Warriors should exhibit the best qualities among men. The true warrior makes a firm decision to try to perfect his character and to live by a strict code of ethics. His word is his honor. His duty stays fresh in his mind. He lives life a little more seriously than most, but at the same time lives life to its fullest. He sees through the veil of appearances covering most parts of this world, but does so without looking down on those who are less perceptive.

Family and friends are important to him, and they know they can always count on him for protection and help in their time of need. He bases his decisions on his code of honor, and because of his training, he instinctively knows right from wrong, and chooses what is right. He knows that at times there is a difference between what is right and what is legal, and what is wrong and what is illegal. As Lao Tzu taught, "Highly evolved people have their own conscience as pure law."

The true warrior is able to hold his head high with honor because he knows that he lives his life authentically and to the best of his ability, with honor and integrity. His code is ingrained in his spirit and is a part of his being. Warriors walk alone much of the time, as they prefer solitude to the company of lesser men. The warrior is a man who aims for excellence in everything he does. These are the things which make someone a true warrior and the development of these traits leads one to live the warrior lifestyle."

That is a good overview of the warrior lifestyle, or as Musashi put it, the way. Once you take your character and honor more seriously, and you start living the warrior lifestyle, you will not want to stray from the way. That is when the principles of the *Dokkodo* will naturally be integrated into the way you live your daily life. In addition, your way and the way of the warrior will become one. Never stray from the way of the warrior!

One must make the warrior walk his everyday walk.
Miyamoto Musashi

Miyamoto Musashi Quotes

Today is victory over yourself of yesterday;
tomorrow is your victory over lesser men.

Get beyond love and grief; exist for the good of man.

Study strategy over the years and achieve the spirit of the warrior.

If you wish to control others, you must first control yourself.

I choose to live by choice, not by chance.

Control your anger. If you hold anger
towards others, they have control over you.

You must understand that there is more
than one path to the top of the mountain.

When you attain the way of strategy, there will not
be one thing you cannot see. You must study hard.

The true science of martial arts means practicing
them in such a way that they will be useful at any time,
and to teach them in such a way that they will be useful in all things.

If you know the way broadly, you will see it in everything.

Do nothing which is of no use.

Never accept an inferior position to anyone. It is the
strongest spirit that wins, not the most expensive sword.

Anyone can give up; it is the easiest thing in the world to do.
But to hold it together when everyone else would
understand if you fell apart, that is true strength.

The ultimate aim of martial arts is not having to use them.

Miyamoto Musashi Quotes

You must not be influenced by the opponent.

Do not regret what you have done.

Your opponent can dominate and defeat you
if you allow him to get you irritated.

The approach to combat and everyday life should be the same.

To win any battle, you must fight as if you are already dead.

A man cannot understand the art he is studying if
he only looks for the end result without taking the
time to delve deeply into the reasoning of the study.

The way is in training.

The way of the warrior is resolute acceptance of death.

It may seem difficult at first, but everything is difficult at first.

The path that leads to truth is littered with the bodies of the ignorant.

There is nothing outside of yourself that can ever enable you to get
better, stronger, richer, quicker, or smart. Everything is within.
Everything exists. Seek nothing outside of yourself.

One thousand days of lessons for discipline;
ten thousand days of lessons for mastery.

You can only fight the way you practice.

If there isn't discipline, how can there
be a true realization of an ideal?

One must make the warrior walk his everyday walk.

Miyamoto Musashi Quotes

Truth is not what you want it to be; it is what it is,
and you must bend to its power or live a lie.

The purpose of today's training is
to defeat yesterday's understanding.

In time, all things work to your advantage
when you pursue them with an open heart.

If you do not control the enemy, the enemy will control you.

In battle, if you make your opponent flinch, you have already won.

In fighting and in everyday life, you should be determined through calm. Meet the situation without tenseness, yet not recklessly, your spirit settled, yet unbiased. An elevated spirit is weak, and a low spirit is weak. Do not let the enemy see your spirit.

Really skillful people never get out of time,
and are always deliberate, and never appear busy.

The important thing in strategy is to suppress the
enemy's useful actions, but allow his useless actions.

The only reason a warrior is alive is to fight,
and the only reason a warrior fights is to win.

To become the enemy, see yourself as the enemy of the enemy.

When you decide to attack, keep calm and dash in quickly,
forestalling the enemy…attack with a feeling of
constantly crushing the enemy, from first to last.

Most warriors only perform tricks.
The way of the warrior is filled with soul and feeling.

Miyamoto Musashi Quotes

Accept everything just the way it is.

The warrior's way is the twofold way of pen and sword,
and he should have a taste for both ways.

Do not think dishonestly.

Become acquainted with every art.
Pay attention even to trifles.

When the enemy attacks, remain undisturbed, but feign weakness.

You always want to lead the enemy about,
rather than be led about by the enemy.

All men are the same except for their belief in their own selves,
regardless of what others may think of them.

Develop intuitive judgment and understanding for everything.

When you attack the enemy, your spirit must go to the extent
of pulling the stakes out of a wall and using them as spears.

No fear, no hesitation, no surprise, no doubt!

Do not let the body be dragged along by mind
nor the mind be dragged along by the body.

With your spirit open and unconstructed,
look at things from a high point of view.

You must cultivate your wisdom and spirit.

Perceive that which cannot be seen with the eye.

It is wrong to be inflexible.

Miyamoto Musashi's Writings

(In the order which they were written)

1) Keidokyo (Mirror on the Way of Combat) 1605

2) Heiho-kakitsuke (Notes on Combat Strategy) 1638

3) Heiho Sanjugo-kajo (Combat Strategy in 35 Articles) 1641

4) Goho-no-Tachimichi (The Five Direction Sword Pathways) 1642

5) Gorin-no-sho (The Book of Five Rings) 1645

6) Dokkodo (The Path Walked Alone) 1645

For My Readers

Thank you very much for your support! I hope you thoroughly enjoyed *Musashi's Dokkodo: The Way of the Lone Warrior* and found it helpful and thought-provoking on your journey.

As you probably know, good book reviews are vital to independent authors and publishers. If you enjoyed *Musashi's Dokkodo*, please take a couple of minutes to review it on Amazon and your social media accounts for me.

Also, follow me on Facebook, Instagram, LinkedIn, and Medium for many great articles and daily motivation and inspiration. You may also want to sign up to follow my website, **TheWisdomWarrior.com**, for news and insightful articles. And be sure to check out the other books from Kaizen Quest Publishing; I think you will find them insightful.

Thank you so much for your time and support!

Bohdi Sanders

About the Author

Dr. Bohdi Sanders is a multi-award-winning and bestselling author. His books, *Modern Bushido: Living a Life of Excellence* and *Men of the Code*, both hit #1 on Amazon. Ten of his other books have also been best-sellers and were also ranked in the Top 10 on Amazon. Dr. Sanders has been a martial artist for over 40 years and has trained in Shotokan Karate, Krav Maga, and Escrima with noted martial artists Master Bob Allen, Shihan William Jackson, and Sifu Al Dacascos. Dr. Sanders is a 5th degree black belt in Shotokan Karate. His work has won several national and international book awards and has reached martial artists throughout the world. He is the author of:

- *Modern Bushido: Living a Life of Excellence*
- *Men of the Code: Living as a Superior Man*
- *Warrior: The Way of Warriorhood*
- *BUSHIDO: The Way of the Warrior*
- *Defensive Living: The Other Side of Self-Defense*
- *The Warrior Lifestyle*
- *The Art of Inner Peace*
- *Secrets of the Martial Arts Masters*

Dr. Sanders' books have received high praise, and he has won several national and international book awards, including:

- NIEA Awards 1st Place Winner: *The Art of Inner Peace* 2022
- BIBA Awards 1st Place Winner: *The Art of Inner Peace* 2022
- #1 New Release on Amazon.com: *Secrets of the MA Masters* 2018
- #1 Bestseller Amazon.com: Men of the Code 2015
- #1 Bestseller Amazon.com: *Modern Bushido* 2013
- The Indie Excellence Book Awards: 1st Place Winner 2013
- USA Book News Best Books of 2013: 1st Place Winner 2013
- The Indie Excellence Book Awards:1st Place Winner 2010
- USA Book News Best Books of 2010: 1st Place Winner 2010

<u>**Other books from Kaizen Quest Publishing**</u>

Made in United States
North Haven, CT
31 March 2024